BigShots' Bull*!@#

The All-New Edition

Deception, Deceit, Disconnect, and Duplicity in the Corporate Sewer

Bonus: four sure-fire sniff tests

By Pete Geissler

ISBN-13: 978-1514395660
ISBN-10: 1514395665

Cover image:
Corporate Bull. Luisa Pizza/iStock by Getty Images.
The Expressive Press purchased Standard License. Order# 26557063

Books from Pete Geissler

- The Power of Writing Well
- The Power of Being Articulate
- The Power of Ethics with Bill O'Rourke
- The Power of Dignity
- Divorce can be Such Sweet Sorrow

Books from The Expressive Press

- VB.Net Web Development by Dr. Charles Wood
- The Little Black Book of Human Resources Management by Barry Wolfe

"Pete Geissler has written bullshit about bullshit, a rare and monumental feat for anyone other than a long-time practitioner. Read, laugh, cry, and resonate with an expert ... all at the same time." A reformed corporate exec and former perpetrator who prefers to hide his identity.

"To my everlasting shame and our mutual fiscal gain, I've collaborated with Pete Geissler to write and disperse millions of words that were masked as marketing, but were really bullshit at its rankest. Readers will be enlightened by the best practitioner of the era." A former manager of marketing communications for a Fortune 100 manufacturer.

PLEASE: Stop here before reading further.

Here are important caveats, warnings, disclaimers that can save my ass and add to my credibility and your enjoyment.

You see, I earn a few shekels by writing, teaching writing, and selling books to businesspersons who wouldn't dream of bullshitting me or anyone else--I am proud to call them my clients and, in my more facetious moments, members of my fan club. I think that they are in the 98% majority of all businesspersons (please note that I did not include politicians), although I just made up that statistic and maybe it should be in Chapter 21. You may have your own guesstimate, and I hope that you'll tell me what it is after you've read the book.

I also am quick to drop clients who bullshit me. You know, the kind who tell me they want to use my services but never get around to writing the purchase order (common), or who promise to pay and don't (rare). They are in the 2% minority and are to be sniffed out and shunned ASAP and at any cost, which I do. But they do have a function in my life: They are my endless source material for this book, one reason I could write it for decades and never, ever get to the last page.

Ah, but I did, which reminds me of the married couple approaching their 90s who told a lawyer they wanted a divorce. The incredulous lawyer asked why, and was told: "enough is enough".

Yeah, Ok, but I know I can't resist a sequel. It's too easy, and too much fun to bash the 2%.

Enjoy and resonate; that's my fondest hope. My second-fondest hope is that your clients are as honest and forthright as mine.

Pete Geissler

Table of Contents

OTHER PUBLICATIONS BY PETE GEISSLER, all available
from **www.TheExpressivePress.com.**

The Power of Being Articulate
The Thoughtful Leader's Model for Wealth And Happiness

The Power of Dignity
The Thoughtful Leader's Model for Attracting and Keeping
Stakeholders.

The Power of Ethics
The Thoughtful Leader's Model for Sustainable Competitive
Advantage.

The Power of Writing Well
The Thoughtful Leader's Model for Business and Technical
Communications.

Beware.

This book can change the way you listen to BigShots—mostly
businesspersons with a snapshot or two of politicians---as they
pontificate for public consumption and personal gain. You'll
recognize the spin, that dastardly polite euphemism for lies that the
advertising/PR folks coined years ago to anoint their profession
with a bit of undeserved dignity. In the process you might gain a
more realistic grasp of what's going on around you and how your
mind is being manipulated, a.k.a. brainwashed.

In all modesty, you're in good hands; some would say the best,
which could be considered bullshit in itself: Who decides?

I would be first in line for an honorary doctorate in bullshit if, by
some stretch of academic chutzpa, it were tendered by any of the
world's great universities. (Actually, I could easily make the case
that degrees in Business Communications or Political Science are
really degrees in bullshit, but that's another book.) I am a master at
crafting bullshit and you, dear reader, will do well to listen to me.
I've written millions of words—speeches, strategic plans, articles,
and all sorts of marketing lies and spins that I too politely call
corporate gargle. I've done that for a gaggle of executives who toil
for businesses large and small, manufacturers and service
providers, technologists and accountants. I've been practicing this
dark, draconian art, and teaching others how to follow my lead, for
40 years, and, as I say jokingly, it shows in my wrinkled face and
cynical attitude that I, with a straight face, call realistic, a true
reflection of the world.

You'll laugh out loud many times as you wander through these pages. My cheeky, witty, acerbic, in-your-face style is sprinkled with the irony of a true gadfly. You'll resonate—see yourself and your bosses in many of my damning examples as clearly as if you had lived them …

…which is surely one sign of a book worth reading, I shit you not.

This is wicked, irreverent entertainment with a serious purpose: to expose the bullshitters around us and bring them to their knees in true penance and supplication. I might say that the book itself is bullshit, that the medium is the message. I could be right. You can decide for yourself.

Enjoy, and always remember these words of extreme sagacity from the rich, dead, and famous:

"Lord, Lord, how this world is given to lying!" William Shakespeare, in *I Henry IV*. Who can argue with The Bard?

"If you can't convince them, confuse them." Harry S. Truman, one of only a few Presidents who knew that the buck really did stop at his desk.

"Bullshit is the primary product of the Information Age." Anonymous, but, in a frequent moment of bullshitting, I claim it for my own.

"Bullshit is the greatest management tool since the pie chart." Also attributed to me, but who the hell knows?

Pete Geissler

CHAPTER 1: BUT FIRST
The Only BigShot Speech that's Totally Free of Bullshit...

The scene: The annual meeting of a large corporation held in the ballroom of a major hotel in Headquarters City. The attendees, except for a few journalists sniffing for another scandal from which they can become the second Woodwards and Bernsteins, are all stockholders or stockholders by proxy-- investment managers and analysts-- and include employees, customers, government officials, and suppliers. The CEO opened the meeting.

Good morning, and thank you all for attending this important meeting of the owners of ABC Corporation.

As I'm sure you're aware, our company's revenue grew last year by five percent, and profits by seven percent—both records for which your managers are justifiably proud. However, both were below analysts' estimates that, I must admit, I said at the time were accurate. So the price of our stock dropped by more than ten percent, and we're all a little bit poorer now than we were at this time last year.

Nobody is more disappointed with the price drop than your top managers and the members of your board. We all have the strongest and most personal interest in market performance.

For example, I will retire in only nine months and I need all the money I can grab if I'm to maintain my lush life style. You probably have no idea how expensive it is to own a home near my country club in the mountains just east of here. Not to mention my chalet in Aspen and my condo in New York, where the old masters you stockholders bought for my enjoyment and to impress other CEOs grace the walls. You should see the spot I've reserved for a

Picasso I've had my eyes on for years. Hey, if my friends from TYCO can collect art at stockholders' expense, so can I. It only seems fair.

So here I am, faced with the tough decisions again, and you who know me know that I won't turn my back on them. Therefore, in order to raise the price of our stock and, not incidentally, the value of my options, which, as you know, are a big part of my compensation and retirement package and have been backdated to be an even bigger part, I am now ordering that we rightsize the company by firing...er, I mean laying off—what the hell is the correct term these days?—ten percent of our workforce. That's across the board, regardless of talent or need or time with the company.

Did I say across the board? A slip, I assure you. Your board will grow from twenty-three of my closest yes-men to twenty-seven, and their pay for each of the three meetings per year will increase from ten to thirteen thousand dollars. Plus expenses, of course. We need to pay competitive fees to attract top talent.

Rightsizing will save your company more than one hundred million dollars per year, and so what if I've destroyed millions of lives and thousands of families—yup, I've even made sure that any number of children won't go to that prestigious university they've dreamed about.

And so what if we forgot that when we hired these people we also were rightsizing. We needed them then to grow, and who knows, we might need them to grow in the very near future. After all, they are our most important assets. Or were, to be precise.

Perhaps the biggest "so what" of the year is simply that you and I know for sure that rightsizing won't work for more than a few months, maybe a year. After the initial drop in costs and rise in profit and stock price, we'll be right back where we started. I couldn't care less; by that time my relatives and cronies, er, fellow managers, and I will have cashed in our options and will leave the mess for whoever is next in the executive suite—assuming, of course that there'll be a business to manage.

Some free advice. If I were you, I'd wait six months or so and then sell my stock. That'll be its high for the year. Guaranteed. I know that I'll be selling then. And you suppliers out there: Find another buyer for whatever it is you're selling. And you politicos—get ready for a new tax base. You get the idea. You can't depend on good old ABC any longer. I'll see to that!

And now, some unsettling news. We still aren't a great company. We haven't moved from good to great, and I can't tell you why because I can't even tell you what those words mean. So maybe we have made the transition after all. Hmmm.

Here's some news that I'm sure you'll all cheer. My total compensation package is now 400 times the average compensation for all employees, and your other managers, including my mistress, your VP of communications who was a secretary only two years ago, are paid handsomely as well.

I assure you that these pay packages are realistic and appropriate in today's competitive environment. Believe me, the competition for top talent is fierce, and we need top talent if we're to raise the price of our stock to where it belongs. Yeah, I know—companies such as Whole Foods limit their CEO's pay to 14 times the average employee's, and their profitability and market performance makes us look like we are managed by monkeys, but, hey, we top guys need the dough to keep up with each other.

For you who are thinking, the answer is 'yes', we still believe in pay for performance. I've already mentioned one example, your VP of communications, who does double duty as my trusted adviser and travels with me everywhere. Another is her husband, a brilliant engineer who I've just appointed manager of one of our largest and fastest-growing divisions, jumping at least four levels and demoralizing the many competent managers who thought they had a shot at the job.

By the way, I was forced to fire one of our EVPs, the one who managed the fastest-growing, most profitable, and largest group in our company. You're right to ask why. Well, he was so outspoken against my enlightened policies that he became a real pain in the shitter and impediment to progress—I need to be surrounded by agreement, not debate. I'm sure that you can see the logic in that.

Now, before the meeting moves on to ten minutes of your pointed, planted, watered-down questions—are the shills in place?—I see great things ahead. We've set stretch goals which all of your top managers have agreed are realistic—revenue up ten percent, profits up fifteen percent, and a new high for our stock price. We can do that with increases in productivity from our dedicated and frightened employees who can shed a little more blood for our benefit. We also will empower them to take risks and make the decisions they're best qualified to make, and encourage creativity and entrepreneurship by creating a culture of fear.

We aim to prove that you *can* get blood out of a turnip, even a frightened one.

Oh, for you who are interested, we haven't forgotten the need for quality products by any means. So the first factory manager who ships out junk just to meet his sales goals for the accounting period will be rewarded with a huge bonus, then promoted to his next level of incompetence. Lord, how I *love* that Peter Principle!

Any questions? Oh, I see that there aren't any, so I move that we adjourn so that we can all make our tee times ...oops. I see a hand waving at me. Yes?

Q. Are you and your cronies enjoying your outlandish salaries? I'm only interested in your happiness.

A. Ah yes, thank you. First, we don't think our salaries are outlandish; we work hard and make the tough decisions. For example, just this morning we as a group decided where you stockholders will be eating your box lunch. Another question?

Q. Are you enjoying your affair with the veep you promoted? I'm also only interested in your happiness.

A. Why, how impertinent. You are out of order. I cannot dignify your question with an answer, and suggest that we adjourn. Will someone so move?

*   *   *

This bullshit-free speech is so real that I'll never be asked to write it or one like it and you'll never be asked to hear it. Nevertheless, I hope that reading it has given you a chuckle or two and raised your awareness of the bullshit that surrounds us like dense and poisonous smog. It also demonstrates with reality, the anti bullshit, many of the topics that comprise the remainder of the book, topics such as Pay for Performance and Jargon.
Read on for more.

CHAPTER 2: DETECTION
If it Walks Like a Duck ...

I am totally convinced that the global institution that we call business can save the world from many of its many ills.

I have my reasons, none of which I think of as bullshit. I believe that business is by far our most powerful single institution, more powerful than government, and I want to tell you skeptics why I think that way. We all interface with and participate in business every day, and it rules our waking hours like no other institution, although I must admit to my horror that government is catching up.

Business is the dog that wags the tail of government, or, if you disagree, perhaps you'll agree that it should and can be. And business adds to its clout every day by hiring lobbyists to sway government. Backroom bribery is a billion-dollar business in itself, and the bribers (business) and bribees (government) are equally to blame for this huge drain on our economy that you and I are forced to pay for with our taxes and higher prices for goods and services. I can easily believe that both sides prefer it that way, simply because both sides pocket big bucks.

So I ask you and myself: How can we harness this very potent and very tarnished institution called business to change the world for the better? How can we convince business to lead the way to a society that is more ethical and responsible and creative? How can business be less exploitive of humanity and our environment?

We can all start by remembering the positive side of business, a side that has been buried by the socialist-hugging media, and, I fear, by the vast and silent majority of businesspeople themselves. Business has been the driving force behind the spread of democracy, and it has increased the wealth and standards of living for millions. It has helped to expand the availability of education for other millions, and diversified economies on local and larger levels. On balance, very few people, even the staunchest socialists, a.k.a. liberals, progressives, left-wingers, and commies, if they could be honest and free themselves from their dogma, would doubt that business has been a very positive force in bettering the human condition, perhaps the most positive in history. I am reminded here of Winston Churchill's remark that "some see private enterprise as a predatory target to be shot, others as a cow to be milked, but few are those who say it is a horse pulling a wagon." I love the horse.

For support, I quote Will and Ariel Durant, in their book, *The Lessons of History*, page 58: "The capitalist, of course, has fulfilled a creative function in history: he has gathered the savings of the people into productive capital by the promise of dividends or interest; he has financed the mechanization of industry and agriculture, and the rationalization of distribution, and the result has been a flow of goods from producer to consumer as history has never seen before. He has put the liberal gospel of liberty to his use by arguing that businessmen left relatively free from transportation tolls and legislative regulation can give the public a greater abundance of food, homes, comfort, and leisure than has ever come from industries managed by politicians, manned by governmental employees, and supposedly immune to the laws of supply and demand. In free enterprise the spur of competition and the zeal and zest of ownership arouse the productiveness and inventiveness of men ..."

As we remember the positives, we cannot forget the negatives. The history of business is blemished severely by extreme degrees of human exploitation such as slavery and union- busting. It is also blemished by greed such as displayed by the robber barons of the early twentieth century and that is continuing today with the exorbitant compensations of BigShots regardless of their competencies, social consciousness, or apparent indifference to protecting the environment. Ironically, all of these negatives have invited government control, just what business wants to avoid, or, in a perfect example of bull, says it wants to avoid. Perhaps the dicey relationship between business and government is best summed up by Will Rogers: "The business of government is to keep the government out of business—that is, unless business needs government aid." I refer you to General Motors, Chrysler, Citi Corp, and others that were 'saved' by my and your generosity forced upon us by a bullying and misguided government.

Business today is saddled with another great negative:

Deceit, a.k.a. bullshit, and it is inviting government control as I write this, and as you can read about later. I believe that such control is just getting out of the starting gate and a plethora of laws is in the wings, waiting for the proper moment and administration in Washington D.C. and in all our state capitals.

Business can put the brakes on this unwanted movement by immediately embracing:

Reality, the anti-bullshit.

I devote considerable ink in this book to defining bullshit as the poison that can kill business. Now I'll devote considerable ink to defining reality, the antidote to bullshit that can revive business.

Reality is truth, yes, and far more. It is what exists; it is actuality, fact, genuineness, authenticity, integrity, and honesty. It is, above all, complete responsibility for individual actions, and how individual actions affect the immediate organization, everyone who is part of it, and the whole of society. It is a total lack of pretense.

Reality is, in the context of this book, one step toward removing the many blemishes on the face of business that are chronicled in this book and that are caused by bullshit. Consider that reality would eliminate false and misleading advertising and public relations, accounting frauds for self enrichment, ethics violations that are justified because the acts are legal, huge payments to BigShots for management failures, justifying firing employees with such euphemisms as downsizing and rightsizing (which manifest management failures), and so on, as you'll read.

Perhaps reality is best defined by that old saying:

If it walks like a duck, swims like a duck, and quacks like a duck, it is a duck.

If business wants to save itself and to lead the way to saving the world, a good start would be to become passionate advocates of reality, and act like an authentic, genuine duck. Is 'save' overly dramatic? Not if you consider that reality and its closest relatives, truth and trust, are at the heart of all human relations, a thought that I reiterate often in this book.

I am not alone in advocating such a novel idea. Philosopher Bernard Gert (1934—2011, former Professor of Intellectual and Moral Philosophy at Dartmouth College), for example, lists, in *The Moral Rules: A New Rational Foundation for Morality,* the ten fundamentals that guide contemporary life. I've highlighted those that apply most vividly to the precepts of this book as seven **Don'ts:** kill, cause pain, disable, deprive of freedom or

18

opportunity, deprive of pleasure, *deceive,* or *cheat.* The list continues with three *Dos: Do keep your promise*, *obey the law*, and do your duty.

Theologian Hans Kung (1928—President of The Foundation for Global Ethics) examined the common teachings/commands of all religions and found five, all of which have countless applications in our society, including in business and politics. Do not kill, *lie, steal, or practice immorality,* and respect parents and love children.

 Rushworth Kidder, in his book *Shared Values for a Troubled World: Conversations with Men and Women of Conscience,* notes five core values: love, *truth, fairness,* freedom, and unity.

And business people worldwide, in survey after survey, list truth, responsibility, respect, and fairness as the most desirable traits of managers, presumably including themselves.

The cynics among us suggest that the survey results are just another example of the hypocrisy behind the words, that BigShots don't "walk the talk". The chasms—I often call them disconnects--that seem to separate words from actions is merely another form of bullshit. In other words, the values they espouse do not align themselves with actions; there are palpable disconnects between the two.

The realists think more kindly of their fellows; they know that the vast majority of businesspersons—I've heard estimates as high as 98 percent—really do believe that their survival depends on truth and trust, and behave accordingly.

Which side are you on?

*　*　*

Is it possible to embed reality as the Next Big Thing in business? On the "yes" side, BigShots will jump on the next bandwagon if another bigger shot starts the wagon rolling by saying it's a good thing. So, all that's needed is a Bill Gates, Steve Wozniak, Lee Ioccocca, Jack Welch or equivalent to say the right words. You can read more about this phenomenon later.

On the "no" side: embracing reality as a new mantra admits to the world that reality hasn't been a top priority in the past, that BigShots have slavishly but erroneously avoided it. Many of the BigShots I know have egos so large that they can't or won't admit to a mistake of any magnitude, much less to one so huge and blatant.

*　*　*

I concluded many years ago that neither I nor anyone else has the *one right way* to address any issue, solve any human problem, resolve any human condition, particularly one as sweeping as the one I discuss in this book. I am far too intellectually humble for such a stance, and I am embarrassed when confronted with the intellectual arrogance of those who profess to know the answers to any and all human conditions. You can only imagine how embarrassed I am with the self-serving pronouncements of our politicians of any party or affiliation, or of self-appointed "experts" on such topics as energy and the environment.

However, I do know that history teaches that there have been many wrong ways to address a host of varied issues, and several right ways are needed that work together toward a solution that works.

For example, we know that there is more than one way to protect the environment, to teach and learn, to manage a company, to govern, to meet our needs for energy, to create a happy marriage or any other relationship, and so on. So Reality isn't the sole way to change the image and role of business. But …

… it surely is a start in the right direction.

* * *

We in business can, without doubt, easily create an airtight case that bullshit is bad management.

We can also create a compelling case that reality is good management, although it's not as simple as creating the case that bullshit is bad. The media avoid reporting the good side of anything, so we're stuck with our own experiences. Here are some of mine--folks and companies that I call the unsung heroes of the business world:

Whole Foods thrives in a culture of inclusion of all constituents, and it does that largely by communicating clearly and honestly. The result is a team of loyal employees and suppliers who work toward common goals, and their stock performance is enviable. Whole Foods has demonstrated that compassion for people and the planet is not only compatible with financial success; *it is the driver behind it.*

Another example is Berner International, the world's largest maker of air curtains, those sheets of air that you walk through as you enter or leave stores at a mall, for example. Georgia Berner, its president and majority owner, wouldn't dream of lying to any of her constituents. In fact, she tells stories about how telling the truth initially shocked customers—she told one, for instance, that her products weren't the best for his application and declined to bid or a large contract. The customer was so impressed with her honesty that, a short time later, he asked her to design a product just for his application, and paid the development costs. He wanted to do business with integrity.

I could tell so many anecdotes about the realities practiced by Jim Browne and his staff at Allegheny Financial that they would fill an entire chapter. Suffice to say that his employees and customers know exactly where he stands at all times, and he won't be associated with anyone who isn't as forthright. His company is growing steadily based almost entirely on referrals and wholly around his core business of financial management.

I know that Ken Lovorn, the owner of a small engineering company that bears his name, couldn't lie and get up in the morning; his company "can't keep up with the work". Jim Nairn, a founding partner in Civil &Environmental Consultants, a larger engineering/consulting company, preaches integrity incessantly; he is hiring and opening new offices as his competitors shrink and wonder what hit them.

Reality is good business, good *for* business and good for all of us.

CHAPTER 3: EPIDEMIC
You Can Run, but You Can't Hide ...

I decided to write BigShots' BullShit because I'm constantly bombarded via the airwaves, the boob tube, and the print jockeys with an unending source of material, really good material at that. Bullshit is the main product of this Information Age in which we live, and it's become a leading—some cynics might say the only-- tool of management in business and government. No writer can resist writing a book when the raw material for it is so plentiful and close at hand; it's almost too easy, and it's certainly too much fun. And it's so hard to finish the book—it is a never-ending labor of love-- simply because new material hits me between the eyes and ears every waking hour.

I presume that the sheer volume and intensity of all the bull around us pisses you off as much as it does me or you wouldn't have picked up this book. Another reason to read this book is that you want to hone your abilities to recognize bull, to separate bull from truth. Perhaps you recognize that your very survival and sanity in this world of swampy, smarmy, misleading, distorted, inflated, obfuscating murk depends on finding some truth around and within your life.

It ain't easy. One reason is that bull shitters are accomplished in their art; they are very skilled at hiding truth because it's in their best interests, a.k.a. more money, to do so. Yes, I'm limiting the gain to big bucks because the end result of all the other 'gains' such as power, prestige, and reelection—even "social good" in too many cases-- is money.

So those other reasons are bullshit in themselves, camouflaged in moral righteousness and superiority. It's the American way at its worst.

Another reason that bullshit is so hard to spot is that it is so polished today that it mixes anonymously with truth, like the cashews that you crave in a big bag of mixed nuts. It's polished because the BigShots hire people like me, a writer with a real and valuable talent, my clients tell me, for extracting the cashews, a.k.a. the essential nuts of a message, and spinning them so eloquently that nobody knows that I have. I'm called a "spin doctor" for good reasons, as are the many other hacks swimming in the same cesspool.

Also, and equally important, BigShots are often sent at the company's expense to 'charm school', where they learn how to deliver a message most smoothly and convincingly. A spun message delivered by an expert equals a double whammy of obfuscation. An aside: I have wondered for decades why a person who can't string together or deliver a coherent speech or sentence is entrusted with running a business or country. I can't wonder too loudly for fear that I will lose my career. You can draw your own conclusions concerning the ethics of that little conundrum. Still another reason it ain't easy to separate bull from truth is simply that we haven't yet defined either term with understandable clarity. Harry Frankfurt tried in his short essay, *On Bullshit,* and failed because he drew the distinction between bullshit and lies so closely that only a professor of philosophy, which he is, can untangle it. His definition also raises the question of why the distinction is at all relevant to anything, much less our lives. Who gives a shit?

Laura Penny, in her screaming screed, *Your Call is Important to Us,* defines bullshit by telling us of two types: Complex and

Simple. Complex "is known as bafflegab or jargon, and it is the native argot of modern bureaucracy. Simple bullshit is all about the dumbed-down, the quick hit, the ad, or the blip on the cable news scrawl."

Like Ms. Penny, I also think that there are two types of bull: committed and omitted. Committed bull is what is said or written. Omitted is what isn't said or written but could be if the perp was at all interested in telling the complete or other sides of a story, which no bull shitter worth his or her salty and forked tongue would ever dream of doing.

All of these attempts at defining bullshit are academic, a.k.a. useless and futile babbling, simply because it's been tried for centuries without a helluva lot of success. The greatest thinkers in history tackled the imposing task of defining *truth* and its opposite, *falsehood*, which we know today by those more politically correct phrases, *I wasn't forthright* and *I misspoke,* and our less elegant word, b*ullshit. Lies* is verboten: it's too direct, too easily understood, so it's politically incorrect, just another way we tolerate perfumed language, a.k.a. euphemism.

The bottom line is simply that we are not blessed with a universal definition of truth or bullshit, just as we are not blessed with universal definitions of many words. If you disagree, gather with your closest friends and try to define liberal, left wing, and progressive (three euphemisms for socialist). Then try to define conservative, libertarian, and right wing (three euphemisms for self reliance and free will). Then, if you get past those hurdles, try to define Democrat, Republican, sustainability (a particularly squishy word that I discuss later), classic, ethics, and morals, and many more of the buzzwords around us that we think we understand but really don't.

25

I tried this enlightening game of defining words that we think we understand with a professor of philosophy and a BigShot in a major company. The conversation stopped just short of blows, their disagreements were so heated. They became totally unglued trying to define *classic,* surely a word without much if any emotional baggage.

I also played the game with three "political progressives" and asked them to tell me the differences between liberals and conservatives. One young lady answered that liberals want to help those in need, and conservatives want to blame those same folks for creating their own problems. When I pointed out that survey after survey concludes that Americans who describe themselves as conservative help those in need by donating more to charities than those who describe themselves as liberals, I was rewarded with the thousand-mile stare. Her mind was locked. And, by the way, none of the three could define *progressive;* one said he "likes the ring of it", as if that has any bearing at all on a definition. I responded, facetiously and with a touch of sarcasm at his stupidity, that I also like the ring of the Liberty Bell and that of my cell phone as it answers a call. I warned you up front that I am a cynic addicted to irony.

Despite our inability to define the term, we "feel" at some intuitive level when bullshit hits our ears and eyes and noses. Some of us feel it more easily and intensely than others. For example, we healthy cynics sense bull more easily and frequently than those of you who are more accepting of the world around you. We call such acceptance *naiveté,* which can be a form of, or a euphemism for, ignorance or stupidity. And it seems to me that we grow more cynical as we age, surely because we have been subjected to more BS over the years. Age also forces the realists among us to realize that we have contributed our share to the din but hate to admit it. I enjoy admitting it—it's cathartic and realistic--so I am the exception.

I am the proud Bull.

A more formal way to spot bullshit is to answer these questions: Who is saying what to whom for what intent and results? Then look for the self-serving biases. A simplistic example would be Senator Weiner and his denial that he twittered his private parts and prurient thoughts to young, attractive women when the whole world was looking at them. He was merely denying the truth (a favorite pastime of pols and other BigShots) to save his marriage and career, and it didn't work, to date, but hold on for more. Other easy examples are the BigShots who plead innocent to accounting frauds in order to paint their businesses as rosy as possible without seeming ridiculous and to avoid being thrown in the hoosegow. The folks at Enron, their accountants, and their cronies at similar firms are good role models for this bit of chicanery, but they have lots of company.

Which brings me to a confession: I toiled for more than 40 years as a writer of what I politely call "corporate gargle", *gargle* being my polite synonym or euphemism for bull shit. Three million words of it at last count, and growing as we speak. So I am a perp in the grandest sense, and I did it for—gasp! — money. I admit to having one helluva good time as well; there's something perversely satisfying about lying, being paid big bucks for it, and knowing that there won't be repercussions of any sort. And I can justify my work in another way by saying that business would be hard-pressed to get its messages out without hacks like me; the bully pulpit of business would be less bully.

27

Maybe you think, as Laura Penny says in her diatribe, that I should be ashamed of my role in spreading bullshit. I'm not and refuse to be. I don't need another guilt trip--my parents gave me more of those than I want or need, as justifiable as this one may be in the eyes of some. We in the business of spreading BizBull can look ourselves in the eye because of the magic of rationalization, that wonderful human trait that preserves our collective sanity by deceiving, a.k.a. bullshitting, ourselves.

Here's how it works. We who toil in advertising/PR often rationalize what we do by saying that informed buyers are able to make more rational purchases when they listen to or read our gargle. But that is bull in itself since our business is to *misinform*—by both commission and omission--so that purchasers are persuaded to make *irrational* choices, i.e. those that sellers want them to make. Go figure.

So let's simplify and say that bullshit is lying, plain and simple, whether it's intentional or accidental. In addition, bullshit is the disconnect—the chasm, if you prefer—between what a person says, and what this same person does. I am particularly fond of this definition because disconnects are generally so easy to spot. Good examples: The BigShot who vows to manage strategically (code for the long haul) and then makes decisions to enhance quarterly accounting statements despite obvious flaws. You'll find many similar examples on the following pages. This definition was described eloquently by T.S. Eliot in his 1927 poem *Journey of the Magi*:

Between the idea
And the reality
Between the motion
And the act

Falls the shadow.

Regardless of your definition, BigShots spew bullshit to advance their own self-interest in most if not all cases. And *self- interest* means to gain an advantage of some sort over another person or organization.

Adam Smith, the Scottish economist of the early 1800s, was no dummy when he opined that all people act in their own best interests, and doing so makes a functioning market and functioning society. His precise words, written in his classic tome *The Wealth of Nations,* are "it is not from the benevolence of the butcher, or the baker, that we expect our dinner, but from their regard to their own interest." In fact, the entire idea that we all behave in our own best interests was put forth around the same time by several writers and thinkers as the basis for a social movement called *individualism.* A French settler in the New World, J. Hector St. John de Crevecoeur, wrote, in 1782, in *Letters from an American Farmer,* "We are all animated with the spirit of an industry which is unfettered and unrestrained because each person works for himself."

In 1985, Robert Bellah, Elliot Professor of Sociology Emeritus at the University of California Berkely, and four of his colleagues wrote *Habit of the Heart: Individualism and Commitment in American Life.* In it, the group opined that "By the end of the nineteenth century, there would be those who would argue that in a society where each vigorously pursued his own interest, the social good would automatically emerge."

Communists and their brethren, socialists, liberals, and progressives, all of whom are fixated in their elitist beliefs that a select few in government know each individual's best interests better than the individual does, would disagree. They ignore a simple fact of history: Never has communism or socialism provided the equitable society that it promised, and, in a prime example of bullshitting the historically challenged, continues to promise today.

At this juncture I am compelled to cite Walter Williams, a nationally syndicated columnist and professor of economics at George Mason University: "What goes unappreciated is that socialists and communists have produced the greatest evil in mankind's history ... Nazism, a form of socialism, murdered 20 million people ... the leaders of the Union of Soviet Socialist Republic—Lenin and Stalin and their successors--killed 62 million more ... and Mao Tse-tung and his successors killed 76 million Chinese ...you can bet that Hitler, Lenin, Stalin, and Mao didn't campaign on the promise to kill millions of their own people."

They accomplished all that while promising social equality.

Bullshitting isn't an exception to the rule of self/best interests. In fact, it may prove it. As I mentioned before, people lie, act unethically, and are dishonest to gain an advantage over others, and their egos are so outsized that they don't expect to be caught. You can read about the actions and words of various perps throughout this book. As you do, I hope that you can weep, as I do, that we as a society have stooped so low as to tolerate such chicanery and stupidity in people in which we have endowed some power and control over our lives. I hope also that you can be enraged with all the bull around us, and actually fight back with reality.

Another observation: I think of lying as the heart and soul, the mother lode, behind many of the ills facing our society. I start with distrust and disgust with our leaders and institutions, particularly those in the White House, governor's mansions, legislatures' floors, and corner offices, and continue with all those who will do damn near anything to be there. Then I add unbridled personal and organizational ambition to my list of ills that actually encourage bull.

CHAPTER 4: SNIFF TESTS
  The Nose Knows ...

We're all faced with the very real problem of separating reality from bull: who can/do you believe, and what of what they say can/do you accept or reject? Here are four infallible ways to answer those tough questions:

1. Practice dialectic, the tried and true method that ferrets and tests reality via rational discussion by rational people who can shed their thinking biases and put their brains into neutral for however long they must in order to arrive at logical conclusions. Such discussions are so rare in these days of finger-pointing and self-aggrandizement that I fear that they may never revive. Perfect examples of anti-dialectic include the many talking heads on TV that masquerade as interviews but are really shouting matches with two or more people trying vainly to be heard when the din and acrimony guarantee that none can be. Sadly, the only practitioner of dialectic on TV that I know of was the McNeil-Lehrer Report, and it has gone the way of most sane and reasoned discussions. Many business meetings also tend to be good examples of dialectic simply because one person is usually in charge and is able to direct the discussion, which may also be bias, egocentrism, or sociocentrism at their zenith. Be wary.

2. Understand the elements of critical thinking, a cognitive process that leads to rational decisions and judgments, and reject those persons who violate them, for they are bull shitters. There are at least twenty five elements of critical thinking; I suggest that you read about them in pamphlets published by the Foundation of Critical Thinking, www.criticalthinking.org. Here are the three that I consider most important to your abilities to sniff out the bull:

--Be suspicious of purpose, since the stated purpose is rarely if ever the real purpose behind the message and is, therefore, bull. Good examples in business permeate this book, but they are especially evident in the pompous pronouncements that managing for stockholder value benefits all stakeholders and that downsizing is needed to save the firm, which of course contradicts every BigShot's stance that employees are the firm's most important assets.

--Reject intellectual arrogance, because nobody has a monopoly on the one best solution to any issue and it pays to be wary of the person who says he/she has. Here's just one example in business that I have experienced: I was asked to write ads and brochures for a huge firm that wanted to enter a new market. When I asked what the firm brings to the party, I was told the "we are ABC Corp and that's enough". In essence I was told to build a case out of egocentrism/egomania, which is always unsuccessful. Where's the substance?

--Detect media bias and propaganda, which covers virtually all of the media's pronouncements, a.k.a. lies, which I address later. Examples in business include the innocuous press release. It always presents one side of any story and it's always the one that paints the issuer in the most favorable light; is that egocentrism? Negatives are always ignored, which assures that balanced discussion is ignored. A good example is the electric car discussed later, and the compact fluorescent light bulb.

3. Learn Socratic questioning, which drills down into messages to find the real purposes, assumptions, points of

view, inferences, and implications. I find Socratic questioning to be the close relative of the oriental maxim that you can't understand a subject until you ask "why" or "how" seven times. Terrific examples in business are strategic plans, discussed later. They invariably focus on growth of revenue and profit, and BigShots, when asked "why?" give me the thousand –mile stare as if I was challenging the Business Bible, aka the mantra of most business schools that the purpose of business is to make money, a.k.a. stockholder value. Of course they cannot give the real reason: to grow their span of control and, ergo, their egos and incomes--egocentrism at work.

4. Recognize these fallacies of thinking—a.k.a. ideas that pretend to be logical but really aren't to anyone who can think analytically-- and question those who use them, for they are in the top tier of all bull shitters:

--*Ad hominum* is attacking the person instead of the issue simply because the attacker doesn't know enough about the issue to speak substantively about it. Sadly, our politicians and media at all levels accept this distasteful fallacy and call it negative advertising. The public follows, sheep-like, without recognizing that they are being duped, a.k.a. bullshitted. *Ad hominum* is often cleverly disguised in business. For example, when a BigShot leaves the firm for "personal reasons" or "to pursue other interests", you can bet that the real reason, more often than not, is that somebody on top didn't like the person, not his or her performance, and engineered the exit. I saw it numerous times in my business career.

--*Red herring* is diverting a difficult issue to one that is irrelevant and simpler to argue, and which is the basis for many mystery novels. For example, a business BigShot may state that the firm is environmentally responsible (an overblown or unwarranted generalization, a.k.a. a policy) and, when asked for support, state that the light bulbs in all offices have been changed to fluorescents (which doesn't explain the policy and is a minor and dubious benefit that anybody can understand).

--*Circular logic—a.k.a. begging the question--* supports an argument or position by repeating the claim in different words. In business: "Of course our employees (or customers) are our most important assets because we wouldn't have a business without them."

--*Egocentrism* is the natural tendency to view issues in relationship to oneself, to be self-centered. Managing for stockholder value, discussed later, is a good example.

--*Sociocentrism* is egocentrism taken to the group level. Labor negotiations are excellent examples since unions generally are focused on very real but narrow issues such as wage increases and job security, and companies on broader issues such as profits, stockholder value and, at times, saving the organization (another term for job security for all employees).

Egocentric and sociocentric thinkers strive to gain selfish interests (would Adam Smith be proud of them?) and reinforce their current beliefs; rational thinkers consider the rights, needs, and beliefs of others to arrive at decisions and actions that are beneficial (or at least acceptable) to most or all.

Other fallacies appear throughout this book. Be on the lookout for *bandwagoning* (arguing that a position is correct because so many people have adopted it); *straw person* (purposely misinterpreting an argument to make it easier to attack either the person or argument); *tu quo que* (justifying an action or position by accusing someone else of the same thing, as if that were relevant); and *unwarranted assumptions* (which cannot be supported by solid examples and which are typically based on preconceived notions ingrained by earlier experiences or egocentrism).

CHAPTER 5: ADVERTISING/ PUBLIC RELATIONS
  Artistic License with Reality ...

True story: A client called, asked me to rush over to her offices. Seems some engineers were trying to figure why a long-standing product wasn't selling, and the meeting was at a standstill. No solutions, no great ideas, no nothing. A fresh mind, fresh ideas, were needed, and quickly.

Smelling an opportunity to create substantive bull out of filmy smoke in exchange for my ridiculously low fees (my perception of truth) or ridiculously high fees (my clients' perception of truth), I rushed over. Then, in a plush conference room, I listened, for two long hours, as the engineers talked about the technical attributes of their product relative to similar products offered by several competitors. Then a marketing director joined us and said that the product costs too much to make "in today's competitive marketplace." More bull, of course, because the marketplace is always competitive: it's the nature of a market economy such as ours is purported to be.

Silence as eight muddled minds looked to me for answers. I squirmed and summed up the meeting thusly: "Phasing out or re-engineering your product aren't options, but, let's face it, they're the only realistic ones: Your product doesn't perform as well as similar products from competitors, but what the hell it costs more too. What smart buyer can resist buying an inferior product for a higher price? So our only recourse is to turn two negatives into a positive and convince buyers to ignore the truth by creating another truth that they can't ignore." I wish I could take credit for that approach to marketing, but in truth I can't; I stole it shamelessly from Edgar Shoaff, who said: "Advertising is the art of making whole lies out of half truths."

"How do we do that?" my fellow inmates asked in unison as they smelled salvation.

"We create communications that over-stress the positives and totally ignore the negatives, and we make damned sure that your sales force understands what we're doing. I'll be back in a week with a program and costs." I suggested a perfect example of bullshitting by omission of unpleasant facts, and I perpetuated my crime by not telling them that simple axiom of the bullshitting trade.

Relieved that I had grabbed responsibility from the jaws of indecision and become a modern-day savior of sorts, the others folded their tents and went about their other business of designing and selling products that actually had some merit. I returned to my office and sketched out a program and message that was totally bull and wildly expensive.

I presented it a week later to wild applause, and, I gotta tell you, I didn't propose a thing that I haven't proposed hundreds of times. Did it work? Did sales perk up? Yeah, for a year or so, and then buyers, no dummies, realized that they had been conned and went elsewhere to spend their bucks. Which brings me to another appropriate quote, this from Stephen Leacock: "Advertising may be described as the science of arresting the human intelligence long enough to get money from it."

I have no idea if the costs of the program were ever recovered. I do know that the product finally met its justifiable end and was phased out. Smoke and mirrors can only do so much, and it can't do it twice with the same product. Consumers are too smart to allow that to happen.

The PR hype over nuclear power that hit its peak in the seventies was another perfect example of bull created by omission. The industry's PR releases such as articles in trade and other magazines focused on how the plants work, particularly that they operate very much like conventional coal-fired plants except for one small difference: the heat to make steam is generated by nuclear fission, a.k.a. a nuclear bomb. But, never fear, they opined, the fission takes place in a very robust steel vessel and is controlled precisely by a bunch of stainless steel rods. True, most of the time.

However, the industry avoided the issue of disposing of radioactive wastes, and, if the subject came up for whatever reason, it was deflected by calling it a political issue, not technical. Their reasoning: The industry knows how to dispose of wastes safely and for centuries; all that's needed is for the folks in Washington to get off their asses and pick a site or two.

Well, they did, in 1987, after decades of study: Yucca Mountain in Nevada, and billions of tax dollars have been spent to develop it—all of it now wasted when Obama cancelled the project soon after his first inauguration. Nevertheless, billions more will be spent to close and maintain the facility.

Meanwhile, the wastes keep building up at hundreds of sites around the country, and estimates are that they all won't be "safely" stored at Yucca Mountain or anywhere else for at least three decades, or around 2040 as I write this.

I often wonder if the nuclear power/government/industrial complex would have prospered instead of foundered if it had told the truth about wastes from its onset in the 1950s—if it had cut the bull and laid it all on the line. We'll never know.

Here's a classic story of advertising/PR gone awry: A dog food maker came up with a new formula that the marketing folks were certain would sell like hotcakes. The company spent millions on advertising and public relations, and sales rocketed—for six months—and then crashed. Dogs, unlike the marketing and research gurus, hated the stuff. Why didn't the company know that? Easy: The research guys neglected to test the product on dogs. My sources for that little story swear that it's true; I find it hard to believe, a.k.a. bulllshit.

Nothing will kill a bad product faster than good advertising and public relations. "Good" means, simply, "convincing"; it doesn't mean truth. I repeat: The perception of truth can be truth, and advertising and PR are all about creating perceptions.

The automobile industry perhaps leads the world in misleading advertising. Ads shout "ALL NEW" when the only thing new on the car is the shape of the taillight or slope of the hood. Underneath the shiny exterior lies the same old heart that has been beating there for decades. Chevrolet, as I type this, is spouting huge bull by misleading the ignorant masses that it offers an electric car that spews "zero emissions, zero greenhouse gasses". It's the perfect whole lie cobbled out of half truths: all that Chevy has done –and all electric cars do--is transfer the emissions from the tailpipe to the power plant needed to make the electricity needed to charge the car's batteries. More on that later.

Bull and *unethical* are often inseparable throughout our society, maybe more so in advertisements. In fact, I could make the case that bull causes unethical. For example, a Big Pharma company ran TV ads in which the doctor who invented the artificial heart hawked a drug that lowers cholesterol, and showed him body surfing to demonstrate his robust virility. The ads were pulled when some whistle-blower revealed that the surfer was a body double, and that the good doctor did not practice medicine and wasn't qualified to recommend drugs. Oh well.

The former ads for Safe Auto Insurance are even more distasteful. In them, folks, mostly young, tell the world that they have been in several accidents and been cited for drunk driving and couldn't be insured but they "need" their cars. Safe Auto saved the day by insuring them with the minimum coverage required by law, putting unsafe drivers back on the road and actually encouraging irresponsible behavior. Isn't that reckless endangerment? If responsible drivers are somehow in an accident with one of them, can't they sue Safe Auto? And aren't you laughing at the contradiction, the huge disconnect, between the firm's name and its actions? I want to call the company *Unsafe Auto*. (To its credit, Safe Auto has since changed its advertising to focus, humorously, on how it has cut costs to cut prices for customers.)

And then there's the trade school that advertises that it doesn't waste students' time teaching them such useless skills as writing and reading and understanding great literature such as Shakespeare. This school brags that it sticks solely to the tricks of a trade, like how to solder wires and turn a wrench. The school is proud that its graduates are illiterate and can't think. But hey, they might be employable at some minimum wage, entry-level job, where they probably will stay with other illiterates.

"Advertising is legalized lying." H.G. Wells, 1866-1946, English author.

The codfish lays 10,000 eggs
The lonely hen but one;

But the codfish never cackles
To tell what she has done.
 And so we scorn the codfish
While the humble hen we prize,
Which only goes to show you
That it pays to advertise.

CHAPTER 6: BUDGETS
Use it or Lose it …

My clients often face a dilemma we ordinary folks would love: too much cash in their budgets and too little time to spend it. So they clean out, a.k.a. spend, their budgets every year in two ways. They load me up with billable work every November and December, and they ask me to pre-bill for work planned for the next year, often with bogus invoices. So I am often wallowing in cash on December 30, the end of my clients' fiscal year, and back to normal by June 30, the end of my fiscal year.

How wonderfully convenient for both of us—and probably illegal since the client is avoiding taxes and I am abetting.

Any suggestion that the unspent money in the budget be returned to the company or government agency is ignored for one simple reason: There will be less money to control next year. Managers avoid that at all costs, even though it's obviously good and prudent management, and, in the buzzspeak of the day, "fiscally responsible". The reason: pay scales are often tied to some extent to the amount of money a person has available for investment in the business, and to another extent by the number of people under his/her wing. A bigger budget is a sign of greater responsibility, of greater span of control. So my clients ask for more money in the budget (and, by extension, in their paychecks) for the coming year, pointing to the faux fact that they spent/invested all the available money last year.

Such financial gyrations supposedly spin to a halt by zero-base budgeting, but they don't, at least in my experience. My clients merely list all the projects they plan for the next year, assign a cost for each, and make sure the total is higher than last year's. It's all bullshit operating behind the fog of good, standard, accounting procedures. (Could that be an oxymoron?)

Perhaps business has taken its cue from government, where BullShit Budgeting is endemic to the point where it seems to be part of many employees' job description. Examples abound in the small city that I call home. We recently built a tunnel under a river that nobody, even the government agency that is funding the work, says will serve any useful purpose. So, you might ask, why is the tunnel being built? Because the money to build it is available, and if it's not spent next year's budget will be cut, as any sane person would want. Honestly, that's the reason the government's PR hacks write with a straight pen. By the way, the budget for the tunnel has soared from about $440 million to over $500 million despite a reduced scope of work, and nobody but a few crusading journalists gives a shit. And the agency in charge says that the budget hasn't been exceeded since overruns are being paid from other accounts. That's shameless bull; all the money comes from you and me.

The same irrational reasoning—how's that for a two-word paradox? -- was used to justify construction of a large office building being built by a bank that boasts of its amazing profitability. Trouble is that nobody says the building is needed in this city with a surplus of office space, not even the bank. So why is it being built? It's funded in part by almost $50 million stolen from taxpayers: use it or lose it. Another reason offered by those who are even more realistic: The governor and mayor are buying the votes of the construction workers and endorsements of their unions at my and your expense. What else is new?

I'll bet that similar things are happening in your area; it surely is happening in DC.

All of this reinforces the extreme bullshit of such terms as managing for stockholder value in business --is the bank managing for the good of its stockholders by "investing" in a building that isn't economically feasible? And it mocks fiscal responsibility—perhaps the most oxymoronic of all oxymorons.

"The biggest gap in the world is the gap between the justice of a cause and the motives of the people pushing it." John P. Grier (1914—2002), an astute American journalist whose real name was Dero Ames Saunders.

CHAPTER 7: EMPLOYEES/CUSTOMERS
Assets or Expendables or ...?

I've never met a BigShot who didn't tell the world that his/her organization's most important assets are employees and customers. Many of them actually believe what they say and behave in ways that nurture these precious assets. Others, usually those who make the headlines, don't walk the talk, and behave as if employees and customers are expendable on the same order as facial tissue or baby wipes. They justify their mass firings, a.k.a. downsizing or rightsizing, as necessary cost reductions, a.k.a. profit and options enhancers, to save the company in tight times when the times aren't so tight and profits are just fine, if down a bit. It's all bull for the unbridled ambition I mentioned earlier, and the insane and self-serving drive for stockholder value that I mention later.

Here are just three quick tales of managers who think of their employees and customers as costs. An accomplished engineer I know was employed by and planned to retire from a small privately owned firm. One day the owner decided that profits were too low, and he fired, without cause, the dozen engineers with the longest tenures, and, of course, with the highest salaries. Revenue dropped for a short time, then bounced back; profits soared for a shorter time, and soon fell to below what they were before the bloodletting. I am sad to report that the owner is still in business, struggling to stay there, I hope. By the way, the dozen who were fired tried to file a class-action age discrimination suit, but soon dropped it when they realized that their petition would be tied up in the courts for years.

A salesman of advertising space for a large newspaper developed his territory using his strong skills for relationship marketing. He was thinking strategically; his employer *said* he was thinking the same way, but he was behaving tactically, i.e. for short-term gain. Anyway, the salesman was fired when his managers realized that he had locked up his customers and not having to pay him wouldn't affect revenue much, if at all. By the way, several of his customers recognized his value and offered him a job the day after he was fired.

A communications manager for a Fortune 500 manufacturer was named "Marketing Person of the Year" for creating acceptance of a new product within a nationwide market. Revenues and profits exceeded the expectations of all BigShots, but that wasn't enough to prevent the manager from being fired without cause. He, like the engineers cited above, started to sue for age discrimination but withdrew when he learned the cost and time. He's still looking for a suitable job as I write this, three years after his illegal firing.

Think back to your entry interview before you started your first or current job. If it was anything like mine, and I'm betting it was, the interviewer told you how well the company treated its employees because, after all, there wouldn't be a company without them. He or she supported this generality by explaining the generous pay and benefits package and how much better it is than the package offered by competitors. He or she went on to explain the company's policy to promote from within—"we believe in developing our own talent and future managers"—and its history not laying off even in the deepest downturns.

Now fast forward to your exit interview. If it was like the six I've sat through, it wasn't much different than the entry interview and it galloped along these lines. We've had # good years together; we treated you well and you performed well, but we must part company because only one person can be promoted to the next level, and we decided on (name). Besides, we're in a bit of a slump now and need to rightsize. Sorry; good luck.

In truth, a strong case can be made that employees and customers are the *only assets of any business in the sense that they are the sources of all other assets.* Run down the list of assets in any balance sheet and you'll see what I mean. In short, employees are the source of all products and intellectual properties, and customers who pay for products and services are the source of all hard assets such as factories and computers and offices. Therefore, employees and customers are the sources of BigShots' salaries and lifestyles.

I am totally convinced that the vast majority of BigShots knows this simple fact of business and compassion, and behaves accordingly. However, you and I don't hear about them; they toil without the fanfare of a media committed to tears and fears.

If you would like to read about some of these unsung heroes, I strongly recommend my book, *The Power of Dignity.* In it, I develop the concept completely, and then profile several highly successful managers who live it. My sincerest hope is that all managers everywhere follow their lead.

"So much of what we call management consists of making it difficult for people to work."
Peter Drucker

And this just in my in-box: Unit labor costs FELL by 4.3 percent in the first quarter of 2103 vs. a projected RISE of 0.5 percent. Are employers squeezing employees to work harder and smarter? Are employees doing so because they are scared of losing their jobs? Are employers investing in tools that raise productivity? Your choice.

CHAPTER 8: ENERGY
Populist Bullshit Run Amok ...

The primary task of politicians—I'm tempted to say the *only* task—is first to be elected and then to be reelected, i.e. get in and stay in office; where else can they get such cushy jobs with health and retirement benefits that the rest of us can only dream about? Unfortunately, that mandate to be elected/reelected leads to all sorts of decisions and pronouncements that are far removed from what's good for the citizens and country, much as managing for stockholder value isn't good for stockholders or others who are vested in the firm.

Leading the way these days are the many flaps about energy and the environment, all of which sound great on the surface, but are rotten at their cores.

Energy independence, for example, is the prime culprit and is an impossible dream, one that's been tried and abandoned by many countries, including the USA. Not one of the 190 or so countries on the planet generates all the energy it needs. Denmark comes close simply because it stayed on the course toward independence since the energy crises of the 1970s, while other countries— especially the United States-- strayed, another example of short-term thinking to solve a long-term problem.

Every country depends on others for some part of its energy mix. Even the OPEC countries, with their plethora of oil, depend on others for gasoline. Of course, that doesn't mean that we in the United States shouldn't make independence our goal; we should, and we can get closer if we really want to. But it's classic bullshit to think that total independence is attainable.

Nevertheless, we try with such trickery as Obama's bull about investing $150 billion in alternative energy. When I hear such Pollyannaish crap I first wonder if he knows what alternative energy is—alternative to what? And then I wonder if he knows that the US has invested—a word that implies that there was some return when there wasn't—many billions, perhaps trillions, of dollars to develop non-traditional energy sources (sources other than fossil fuels and uranium) since the first oil embargoes of the 1970s. And I wonder if he knows that our oil imports have grown during the ensuing years from about thirty percent of our consumption to about seventy percent of a much larger total, so the number of barrels we import has soared. And, finally, I wonder if he knows that the several forms of solar energy that we hold so dear, from photovoltaic cells to windmills, provide only a few percentage points of our consumption. And, during a record hot spell in Texas, windmills were able to generate only 880 megawatts of power out of 10,135 megawatts of capacity simply because the winds subsided when needed most. On top of that, electricity from wind costs 150 percent of electricity from traditional sources. Nevertheless, our government is planning to "invest" billions more in this bull that is guaranteed to lower our standard of living and raise its cost.

So, despite all logic, here we are, proving our insanity by repeating history and expecting a different result. Ethanol's lure of being home grown is perhaps the most dangerous delusion and deceit. More oil and other traditional sources of energy are needed to grow the corn and then produce and transport ethanol than ethanol delivers to a vehicle. So it will actually *increase* our dependence on imported oil and has already *increased* the costs of food simply because farmers sell their corn to the highest bidders, the subsidized ethanol producers. Thank you, taxpayers. Senator Kay Hutchison, R., Texas, rightly says that America must undo its "ethanol mistake". But then she wrongly advocates freezing the biofuel mandate at current levels, when we should dismantle, now, all that we've done so far.

Nevertheless, the whole idea of home-grown energy is too enticing for our vote-seeking leaders to resist. The idea is so enticing, in fact, that the former governor of Pennsylvania, the zenith of a self-serving politician, handed $21 million to Getty/Lukoil, a *Russian* oil company, to build an ethanol plant in the center of the state, which just happens to be the center of the state's agriculture industry as well. I guarantee that the governor will brag about the jobs he created with my and your money, when the real reason—gasp!—was to buy farmers' votes.

Hydrogen is actually less efficient than ethanol; it will consume considerably more energy to produce than it delivers. But, oh my, its lure is impossible to resist by the short-term thinkers we call leaders. A friend, a political junkie and intellectual joke, told me that we must develop hydrogen because we have so much of it in the oceans. When I asked him if he knew how hydrogen is extracted from seawater, he said that we just pull it out, voila! So I told him to fill the gas tanks of his two SUVs with seawater and let me know how they run. His silence is a perfect example of uncritical thinking.

The same is true of Chevy's and BMW's claim—and others, including the Federal government's--that the hydrogen car will emit only clear, pure water. BMW at least tries to be honest by saying, in a footnote where only the super-curious will read it, that zero emissions of greenhouses gasses, which they erroneously limit to carbon dioxide, is possible only if the electricity to make the hydrogen is generated by solar energy. At the moment this

51

country doesn't generate enough solar electricity to charge two kids' toys at once, and won't anytime soon; solar just isn't feasible in most parts of the country. And, by the way, water vapor and methane are greenhouse gases too—methane is three times more powerful a greenhouse gas than carbon dioxide -- and they are far more abundant in the atmosphere than carbon dioxide. But they're ignored in the debate over global warming because we can't control them, and our leaders can't make us feel guilty about emitting them. Yes, even Al Gore in all his pomposity cannot prevent cows or termites from farting, but I wouldn't be surprised if he tried.

By the way, both ethanol and hydrogen are very difficult to transport to a local filling station; they'll require a brand new and very expensive infrastructure that nobody wants to mention. Is that a classic case of bullshit by omission?

The electric vehicle is justified with a similar rationale: It will help us reach the Promised Land of Energy Independence and clear the environment of pollution as well. Chevrolet, BMW, Toyota, Nissan, and a host of smaller firms—most located in California, where government has mandated a shifting percentage of cars to be electrically powered in the very near future-- are working mightily to develop this answer to our prayers. So far, prototypes are very expensive and the cars need to be recharged after being driven for only 100 to 250 miles. Forget driving to Grandma's house in the next state for Thanksgiving.

The makers and proponents also don't issue a peep that electric cars consume a great deal of energy in the form of electricity to recharge, and more than seventy percent of that electricity is generated by combusting oil, natural gas, and coal. And they don't tell you that emissions of all sorts of pollutants are transferred from the tail pipes of vehicles to the stacks of power plants, just as they are with the hydrogen car.

Of course, all this bullshit would go away if new technologies were to be developed that eliminated the shortcomings of these and other panaceas. I'm thinking of more efficient ways to produce and transport ethanol and hydrogen, and more nuclear plants to generate electricity.

A quick but important aside: The rationales for both ethanol and hydrogen fuels are red herrings, a form of fallacious thinking I discussed earlier that diverts a difficult issue at hand to an irrelevant issue that has more emotional appeal or is simpler to argue. The main emotional appeal attached to both fuels is that they will rid us of the oil exporters who are gouging us. In fact, both fuels will have the opposite effect, but to see that requires thinking beyond the surface and delves into another form of really bad thinking: politically incorrect or correct, both of which are totally unrelated to "correct" or "intellectually honest".

To learn more about this very important topic, read, *Gusher of Lies: The Dangerous Delusions of 'Energy Independence'*, by Robert Bryce, a free-lance journalist specializing in energy issues. He makes two points that are appropriate here. We import only 11 percent of our oil from Persian Gulf countries (but those countries are blamed most often for all sorts of supply and price ills). And nuclear power is the only sector that has enough momentum and capital behind it to make a significant dent in the overall use of fossil fuels.

"The only means of conservation is innovation." Peter Drucker.

CHAPTER 9: FORECASTS
The Tail is Wagging the Dog; The Answer is Wagging the Question ...

If humans can be certain of anything aside from death and taxes, it's that we cannot predict the future with any accuracy or detail. Our recent past is replete with examples; here are a few of hundreds: *Democracy will be dead by 1950*, wrote John Langden Davies in his 1936 book, *A Short History of the Future*; *Remote shopping, while entirely feasible, will flop*, pontificated Time Magazine in 1966; *It will be years –not in my time—before a woman will become Prime Minister*, said Margaret Thatcher in 1969; *Read my lips; no new taxes*, promised President Bush II in 1988; and so on.

Despite the obvious failings and pitfalls, economists, stock analysts, and just about every businessperson are literally forced to forecast economic activity, generally as a first step in so-called investment or strategic planning. The forecasts may be of a broad section of the economy, such as the world or the country. Or they may be more confined, such as an industry, or even more specific such as a single product or service in a small geographic area.

Regardless of scope or focus, forecasts of economic activity are almost always wrong, a.k.a. full of bullshit. We know that because forecasters are rarely heard crowing about the accuracy of their work, which, being human, they would if they could.

Nevertheless, forecasts are necessary if we are to live, which requires us to predict/project/plan the future either formally or informally. All of us do that every time we shop for anything from a house to a pizza, and when we marry or enter a career or profession, and so on.

Businesspersons generally subscribe to formal projections, a.k.a. computer modeling, which has taken on the aura of scientific numbers-crunching, which has come to represent total objectivity, rationality, and reason. They have become businesspersons' comfort food, therapy, and fallback position (read *excuse*) should things go wrong down the road.

Computer models aren't or shouldn't be any of these things, yet businesspersons want to believe they are, perhaps because many B-schools teach that businesses can be managed well—best? --by the numbers, which never lie, so the results can't be skewed.

They do lie and they are skewed, and here's why. The input numbers, called *assumptions*, no matter how carefully selected, do not consider human emotions such as greed, hatred, avarice, generosity, caution, daring and so on. Nor do they consider unseen events such as 9/11 or violent weather or extraordinary moves by competitors or new technologies. Therefore, every forecast can be matched by an opposing forecast, and by countless others in the middle ground.

For example, back in the 1970s and 1980s the coal and nuclear power folks were saying with absolute statistical certainty that the world would run out of oil in only 30 years, another example of computer modeling gone astray. They were sure that we were on the road to a society without cars, trucks, and light bulbs. They then said that they could save us from this bleak future by generating more electricity using plentiful supplies of coal and uranium.

They couldn't have been more wrong, as we all know by now.

Recommendations to government and to industry, all supported by a raft of graphs and charts generated by the massive computers of the day to prove the objectivity of it all, were to quickly develop known and plentiful resources, especially coal and nuclear, with a touch of alternate sources such solar, largely windmills and photovoltaics. Billions were invested in the insane rush to become energy independent.

Our predictions couldn't have been more wrong. Today, more than forty years later, reserves and demand for oil are both far higher than we projected. The world is awash in oil, and we are using it faster than ever. Projections of when we will run out vary widely, but everyone agrees that we will-—someday. The inevitable result of soaring demand and controlled supply will be higher prices—I make the projection without fear of being wrong, simply because I know that the laws of supply and demand are hard at work. But I will never predict *how* high, simply because neither I nor anyone else can predict the human behavior that will affect demand more than any other factor.

Another example. I have written many strategic plans for Westinghouse, once a major supplier of equipment used to make and use electricity. All depend on assumptions of demand for electricity which are based largely on historical trends. They ignored several conflicting trends that were and remain impossible to predict precisely such as the rising costs of fuel and declining birth rates, which suppressed demand, and rising use of computers and other electronics, which raised demand. The results were plans/projections that were impressive presentations to top BigShots, but were useless as planning tools and were put on the shelf to gather dust soon after they were written. Managers then applied their intuition to the models and decided on plans of action.

Examples on a broader scale abound. Perhaps the most startling has been the failures of communist and socialist countries to plan production that provides goods to citizens in anything approaching adequate quantities or qualities. In our own backyard, the chronic inability of government and private forecasters to see the growth or shrinkage of the GNP, deficits, and other manifestations of our macro economy always astounds and amazes. And the volatile, short-term prices of oil and gasoline can't be foreseen simply because production and prices are controlled by the greed or charity of others.

The combination of mathematical models and intuition as a means to forecasting is called *iliative sense.* It transcends "gut feeling", the approach Bush II espoused and seemed so proud of that has plunged the world into so much turmoil and that is usually based on too few or too biased faux facts. In contrast, *iliative sense* applies and coordinates lifetime experiences with new data to arrive at decisions that are far more likely to be correct than either the numbers or gut feelings. BigShots at every level and in every sphere of life need hard data and soft knowledge in huge doses to arrive at decisions that are "correct" or at least closer to correct than they would be otherwise.

In short, the search for truth, whether we look back to the past or forward into the future, is risky and uncertain no matter how hard we try. But try we must.

"People who don't believe in global warming think the earth is flat." Al Gore

Poor Al; he couldn't be more wrong on all sorts of levels. First, he calls me and countless others stupid—or, in today's parlance, "historically or intellectually challenged"-- because we don't believe (note the word *believe* and not *know)* that the globe is warming, and I have many volumes and statistics to prove/demonstrate that it isn't. By doing so, he alienates many folks and indulges himself in another fallacy of thinking called *ad hominum,* which is the time-worn and downright dirty attacking of the person instead of the issue. Politicians—and Al is one forever-- and others resort to *ad hominum* when they don't have any real and substantive evidence to fall back on; real scientists and clear thinkers wouldn't dream of doing so.

His second wrong is simply that his so-called evidence is so biased that it is unbelievable. His one-sided movie, incredibly, won an Oscar, and he somehow hoodwinked the Nobel Prize committee into an award---a peace award at that, as if global warming has anything to do with peace--all based on bullshit. In the movie, he showed a polar bear on an ice floe as proof that the polar bear population was falling as the arctic ice melted. In fact, the population of polar bears has at least quadrupled in the fifty-plus years since 1960. His extreme bias demonstrates two other forms of fallacious thinking called *a priori judgement* (reaching a conclusion without sufficient evidence) and *ad ignorantium* (arguing that something is valid because it has not been proven wrong).

Perhaps Gore's most egregious fallacy is basing his conclusions on computer modeling, which, as I've pointed out earlier, has damaged our society and economy in countless ways simply because it can be manipulated so easily. For example, and I quote from *Useless Arithmetic* by Orrin Pilkey and his daughter, Linda Pilkey-Jarvis, both scientists of considerable stature:

"Bureaucrats who don't understand the limitations of modeled predictions often use them. That is why the Bureau of Land

Management allowed open-pit mines that, once abandoned, would eventually become giant cups of poison...and fishery models became the fig leaf (cover-up) that allowed Canadian politicians to ignore the dying Grand Banks cod fishery. Agencies that depend on project approvals for their very survival (such as the U.S. Army Corps of Engineers) can and frequently do find ways to adjust models to come up with correct answers that will ensure project funding. Most damaging of all is the unquestioning acceptance of the models by the public because they are assured that the modeled predictions are the state-of-the-art way to go."

In short, modeling has been demonstrated to be bullshit for so long and in so many instances that it should have lost all its credibility years ago. Instead, modeling has become the reason to accept the ridiculous, the absurd, and the hopelessly skewed.

In the case of global warming, the models are polluted and corrupted for political ends and for a host of other reasons. First is an impossible time span of hundreds of thousands of years. (A valid criticism of global warming is that we can't predict tomorrow's weather with precise accuracy, so how can we predict temperatures many thousands of years in the future?) Next, we ignore verifiable history, particularly the record of the Chinese fleets of 1420 through 1423 that supposedly documented that bananas were growing and cattle were grazing in Greenland. Some historians have discredited this "fact" that was put forth in the book *1421: The Year the Chinese Discovered the World,* by Ramon Menzies, and called it "revisionist history", a.k.a. bullshit. I found the book compelling, but I am not a historian and cannot verify its premise. I suggest that you read the book and decide for yourself.

Next we have miniscule, short-term experience in measuring warming or cooling on a global scale—and still don't do that reliably in my view-- so we could very well be magnifying assumptions to the extent that they are meaningless. And last, we have no idea of the interdependence of all sorts of natural and man-made variables. For example, we humans may decide that we can live just fine without our cars and electricity, as far-fetched and idealistic as that may sound at the moment.

Nevertheless, and despite all these shortcomings and fallacies, maybe Al Gore has done us a favor by alerting us to the real need to reduce our consumption of fossil fuels. I could also argue that he has done us a huge disservice by preventing development of oil and coal reserves as we hope for the so-called alternative sources of energy to fulfill their impossible promise.

And, although neither Gore nor any of his followers would ever admit it, Gore followed the second President George Bush. Yes, Bush alerted us to the same need to reduce our oil consumption when he said, in his 2007 State of the Union address, that "America is addicted to oil". He then unveiled an energy plan that fell far short of what was needed. I occasionally wonder why Bush as the pioneer was not awarded an Oscar and Nobel, or, to be totally off the wall, why Gore didn't thank him for leading the way.

And, by the way, Bush, in another shameless capitulation to governing by polls (a form of bandwagoning that I discuss in a later chapter), succumbed to political pressure and agreed with the global warming advocates. Also, by the way, the global warming advocates aren't so sure of their position any more. They've decided to cover any eventuality and switch to "climate change", just in case "the majority of scientists", another pile of bull called an unsupported/unsupportable generalization, changes its mind again—as this amorphous group has six times since 1900--and decides that the globe is really cooling, as they projected in the mid 1970s.

Tell me, if climate change caused by man's activities is a scientific fact, why do the scientists need to hedge their bets? (I feel compelled here to disclose one of the more inaccurate projections of climate change that I know of. A professor at a small, highly respected university said in no uncertain terms, in the mid 1970s, that the United States would be covered by ice and the globe would be eleven degrees cooler by the year 2000. How wrong can one person be?)

I could write a book about this string of hoaxes that could cost our country trillions for absolutely no benefit to either us or the world, but instead I'll refer you to the works of real scientists. Read Michael Crichton's book, *State of Fear;* Dr. Fred Singer's book, *Unstoppable Global Warming: Every 1500 Years;* and Dr. Patrick Michaels' book, *Shattered Consensus: The True State of Global warming.*

And I am struck by this statement from Dr. Orin Pilkey, a scientist and staunch believer in global warming: *"It is easy to understand the basis of skepticism about the human role in global change because what's happening now has always happened. In the past, sea level always has been changing, sometimes at slower rates than at present. Global temperatures and rainfall rates have been higher and lower. Deserts have changed into tropical rain and forests and glaciers have come and gone*

*'What's new is that the human race is here. **If the scientific community is correct***

(emphasis added) we are causing global climate changes to occur rapidly and in a particular direction…"

I wonder if Gore and his sheep-like followers are aware of Earth's history or of the uncertainties that permeate the so-called scientific community. My guess is that their minds are fixed.

My advice to all who are listening:

- ❖ Don't waste your time and predict the future any further than tonight's dinner; we humans can't with any accuracy and our computers won't and can't help, so
- ❖ Adapt as conditions change, just as the human race always has throughout its short tenure on this floating rock that we call home.
- ❖ And consider these thoughts:

"The past is gone; the present is full of confusion; and the future scares hell out of me." David Lewis Stein, former urban commentator for *The Toronto Star.*

"Long –range planning does not deal with future decisions, but with the future of present decisions." Peter Drucker

"Life can only be understood backwards; but it must be lived forwards." Soren Kierkegaard

Just for fun: more wrong predictions: In *The Doomsday Book,* published in 1970, author Gordon Taylor said that Americans were using 50 percent of the world's resources and that "by 2000 (Americans) will, if permitted, be using all of them." Also in 1970, Harvard University Nobel laureate biologist warned:

"Civilization will end within 15 or 20 years unless immediate action is taken against problems facing mankind."

Again in 1970, Senator Gaylord Nelson, quoting Dr. Dillon Ripley, warned that by 1995, "somewhere between 75 and 85 percent of species of living animals will be extinct."

In 1974, The US Geological survey said that the US had only a 10-year supply of natural gas; today we have a 110-year supply and it's growing as we speak.

In 1975, The Environmental Fund warned, in a full-page ad, that "The world as we know it will likely be ruined by the year 2000."

In 1996, Lester Brown, who had been predicting global starvation for 40 years, received a MacArthur Foundation "genius" award, along with a stripend. The foundation had previously bestowed the same award to Dr. Paul Ehrlich, who predicted that millions of Americans would die of starvation. Note that the awards and stripends of $300,000--$400,000 were granted well after the two predictions were proven to be total bullshit.

CHAPTER 10: HONESTY
   Treachery, We've Found, Can Pay ...

I am idealistic enough to believe that honesty is always the best
policy and that it will always pay off in fiscal and psychic rewards.
I also believe that the opposite side of that coin is always true—
that charlatans and bull shitters will always be caught and punished
in horrible ways. To put that ideal in the context of business, I am
convinced that persons with reputations for fair and forthright
dealings will prosper and their firms will be profitable.
Therefore—if I may stretch the logic chain--the most profitable
firms are managed and staffed by honest persons, and the least
profitable aren't.

Unfortunately, I have no proof--and, as far as I can find in my
research, neither does anyone else—that my beliefs are even close
to reality. I cannot prove that honesty and profitability are even
remotely correlated, much less that honesty causes profitability, or,
to put the idea in the passive voice that is so endeared by bull
shitters for its ability to obfuscate the simplest concepts:
profitability is caused by honesty. Nevertheless, I and I hope in my
own naïve way many others, still believe that honesty really is the
best policy and not the bullshit that I fear it has become.

All of this begs the question: Why do so many BigShots bullshit so
much and often? Perhaps because very little in the record indicates
that dishonesty in business—including and especially in the
business of sports--is punished in any way, not by jail time or
lower earnings or being sacked.

Perhaps *very little in the record* offends some readers who are
familiar with the recent Enron, WorldCom, Tyco, Adelphia,
Hollinger, Westinghouse and similar cases in which a few

BigShots were jailed for their deceptions. But, as I point out later in this small book, very few BigShots who were convicted for various forms of chicanery spend more than a few months in jail, and the jail is typically what the hard-core hoods call "soft time".

In addition, those cases amount to the very small tip of a huge iceberg, but, like all tips, they are the only parts of the iceberg that are visible, especially to the sensation-seeking media.

Beneath the surface are countless everyday events that I'm certain you've experienced. Think about the stockbrokers who tout shares in shaky companies and the purchasing agents and salespersons who know that their firms won't or can't live up to the terms of contracts but accept them anyway. Don't forget the real estate agents who knowingly sell defective properties to buyers who can't afford them—did that help to create and then burst the real estate bubble? Then there are the mechanics and home remodelers who recommend unneeded repairs, the used car salesperson who knowingly hides accident records or other defects, and so on and on.

Dishonest businesspersons—and leaders in government-- continue to be dishonest and survive simply because honest consumers, which include those consumers of government called voters, are complacent. Too many of us avoid conflict at almost any cost. Instead of confronting bullshit, we quietly take our business elsewhere, and some of us even move out of the city, county, or country in a futile effort to find more honest pastures, as if there are any. It's so much easier. And it confirms Irish philosopher Edwin Burke's famous aphorism that all it takes for evil (a.k.a. bullshit) to thrive is for good people to do nothing.

Therein lies the rationale for this final thought: *Cases that apparently demonstrate the awful consequences of abusing trust turn out to be few and weak, while evidence that treachery can pay seems compelling.* So says the Harvard Business Review, so you must know that it is reality (sic).

CHAPTER 11: BUSINESS SCHOOLS
If You Can Manage One Business, You Can Manage Any...

The dean of a major business school told me that nothing of practical value and use has ever come out of academia. The ethereal subjects of articles in the Harvard Business Review would tend to confirm his cynicism. Nevertheless, managers at all levels continue to pore over the pages of this and similar journals, searching for the next secret for success much as the folks at cocktail parties search for their favorite appetizers.

They are more likely to find secrets for failure, one of which is the hypothesis—it has yet to rise to the level of theory and is eons away from fact-- that all businesses are managed by the same principles and, therefore, can be managed by any manager who understands these principles.

Bull.

Roger Smith, the former CEO of General Motors, is a good example. He was a financial wiz who came up through the ranks at GM's treasury headquarters in New York. He knew the money side of making vehicles, but, in the words of one journalist, in the business of making and selling cars, he was practically clueless.

His cluelessness is exemplified by a few stats of GM's performance during Roger's nine-year tenure as CEO: Between 1981 and 1990, GM's market share in the US fell from 44 to 36 percent, setting the stage for the firm to lose many billions. He spent billions on acquisitions designed to save the company and didn't, and he formed Saturn to build cars starting from a clean sheet of paper, which angered other managers who wanted the investment dollars to improve their own products. Almost 20 years later, GM was still recovering from Roger's mismanagement, and in 2010 the company was "saved" from bankruptcy by you and me, a.k.a. taxpayers. The Obama administration brags about the number of jobs it saved, but never about the billions of dollars lost as GM's stock price has fallen. And, BTW, Saturn has gone the way of all flesh.

Westinghouse Electric, now a faded memory, is another example. Not satisfied with being modestly successful as a maker of big and sophisticated electrical equipment for utilities and industries, it fell into the trap of diversification as the road to growth and the arrogance of universal management. So it ventured into all sorts of businesses that stock analysts and other gurus had anointed as "growing faster that the GNP": watches, bottled water, housing, robotics, and computers to name a few. Trouble was that nobody in a company focused on industrial markets knew how to manage businesses focused on consumers, so many of the new businesses tanked.

We in the advertising/PR business often jump into the bar/restaurant business as investors, owners, and operators simply because we spend so much time in such places that we think we can run one better than the folks who actually do so—pure bullshit in most cases. A friend fell into that trap and bought a small café about 70 miles from his home, fired the current managers, and took over with all the verve and nerve of a true novice. He soon found that the wait staff—mostly students at the local college-- showed up whenever they damned well pleased, purveyors didn't trust the new guy on the block and demanded payment before delivery, and the chef wouldn't change the menu despite good reasons for doing so. My friend found himself working 80—90 hours a week to pick up the slack of irresponsible employees, and borrowing big sums of cash to pay purveyors. After a year, he was being sued for divorce by his neglected wife and back pay by his disillusioned employees, so he declared bankruptcy, and now you and I are paying for his hubris as we always do when debts aren't paid.

A large engineering/construction company I worked for as a sales engineer remained in business happily for a century by carving out a niche in the steel and iron-mining industries with steady, competent expertise. Then, caught up in the frenzy for growth for the sake of growth, the board hired a CEO, the first ever who wasn't pulled from the ranks of the company and who was an accountant, not an engineer. He immediately diversified into other industries such as power generation and paper that he figured needed the same kinds of expertise. Yes, those industries need engineering/construction services, but from companies and people who understand the businesses and the technologies that support them.

The result was that this firm transformed itself from being well established in a comfortable niche to being just another engineering company. In short, it lost its identity, its culture, its reason for being, its Unique Selling Proposition or USP, as we in the communications business are fond of saying. Management then went on that old familiar spree of buying firms (read egocentrism and bandwagoning) with the needed expertise, and of buying contracts with bids so low that customers couldn't turn them down despite the obvious pitfalls. As is so often the case—the latest stats I've read indicate that more than ninety percent of all acquisitions fail to meet the expectations of the acquirers—the grand old company went belly up, ruining thousands of lives in the ugly process.

There are tricks to every trade. To think otherwise is pure bull.

CHAPTER 12: JARGON
   Useful, Useless, Code for BS ...

BigShots have at their command a vast lexicon that is freighted
with vague and ambiguous meanings, a.k.a. bull shit, when it suits.
Here's a mythical letter or speech to stakeholders that uses many
of those words and muddles any meaning to the message:

*"Your company is fully committed to a proactive, strategically
based, bottoms-up strategy, a platform that will expand the normal
parameters and paradigms of business and frame the dialog for the
foreseeable future. The bottom line is that this actionable, state-of-
the-art agenda—which I see as our wake-up call—is grounded on
solid benchmarks, databases, and anecdotal evidence that are no-
brainers. Our strategy will drill deep into our broad matrix of
assets. For example, our employees will be encouraged to think
outside the box to incentivise and empower them, allowing us to
find target-rich markets and to cherry-pick opportunities and
harvest the low-hanging fruit. We'll milk our cash cows and
exploit our core competencies while we avoid rocking the boat and
any worst-case scenarios such as gridlock. We will never be
circling the drain. In short, we will have the best of all worlds, a
sure-fire win-win.*

*"I can assure you that we'll stay on track and our wheels won't
come off and cause a train wreck as we travel down this value-
added road. We won't crash and burn or look for an exit strategy
as we maximize and leverage our assets and energize our base and
re-purpose our bricks and mortar. On the other hand, we will
actualize our template and our critical mass to revitalize our
infrastructure. I assure you that we will maximize our skill sets.*

"As I envision our scenario, I see that we are on the cusp of a new horizon, the bubble of a new era of world-class prosperity for all stakeholders. We see great upside potential downstream.

"I assure all of you that I will keep you posted on an as-needed basis as we ramp up and enter uncharted territory. We will avoid any disconnects between us."

Every business and profession has its own language (jargon) that allows those in the know to communicate with each other in shorthand, or code. It saves all sorts of time and ink, raising productivity and lowering costs. It is slang, and, as Carl Sandberg said, "Slang is language that rolls up its sleeves, spits on its hands, and goes to work."

A few examples: Westinghouse people referred to manufacturing plants by their locations: "Raleigh" meant the meter plant in North Carolina, and "Lester" meant the turbine plant near Philadelphia. They also referred to "our nukes" as the light water reactors it offers, and "their nukes" as the boiling water reactors General Electric offers. Writers also have their own language. For example, a galley is text ready for printing, not a kitchen on a ship, and "agreement" means the noun and verb in a sentence are both singular or plural, not a pact or meeting of two or more minds.

"The chief virtue that language can have is clearness, and nothing detracts from it so much as the use of unfamiliar words."
Hippocrates (460?—370? BCE)

CHAPTER 13: THE NEWS
  Putting Lipstick on a Pig ...

Maybe it's the cynic in me, but more likely it's my vast and tawdry experience with manipulating the media that makes me believe that the news—including the business news-- is *never* the truth, that it is *always* bullshit, even if the bullshit is, at times, tough to detect. (OK, the so-called straight news—items such as man bites dog, car hits pedestrian, rain continues to fall—aren't skewed)

I have my reasons to think that the news is skewed and examples to back them up. News from the companies I've worked for is:

❖ **Filtered**: A good example is the annual report, BigShots' most important opportunity to crow about their achievements. I can tell you that months are needed to create this simple and short document. One reason: A cadre of BigShot employees examines every word with the greatest care. Start with lawyers to be sure that what's said can't land the firm in court and accountants to be sure that the numbers conform to Standard Accounting Procedures (which are loosely at best related to reality, as any person who has operated a business, as I do, knows only too well). Add into the mix advertising/PR execs to maintain the desired image of the firm, and others such as engineering managers with a vested interest. Filter after filter absolutely guarantees that the content is generalized and watered down, and the result is pap.

The same is true of press releases. The words are selected carefully by PR execs and reviewed by lawyers before being released to the media who dutifully print or mouth them, often without changing a word or checking the facts. Editors love me; the releases I send them are written so well that they don't need to edit them. But they are still bull.

Adlai Stevenson said, "Newspaper editors … separate the wheat from the chaff, then print the chaff." The same is true of radio and TV editors.

BTW, the annual report from Berkshire Hathaway is an exception to my rule: it is refreshingly straight-forward, written in plain language, and entertaining as well. In short, it is an island of reality in a sea of bullshit.

❖ *Simplified*, dumbed down, to make it understandable to the average housewife or Joe with a fifth-grade education, or, as we say in the trade, congresspersons and their aides. I was once asked to write a description of a medical procedure that, in the words of the doctor I worked with, "even the Mayor could understand". I also produced many documents about nuclear power and the energy crisis that turned into comic books that could be scanned in a few minutes so our government officials and their aides could at least get the main points. Much of the same sins are being perpetrated on these same readers by companies and individuals with interests in energy, the environment, and other hot topics of the day.

❖ *Dramatized* to catch readers' attention where it's not warranted. Drama is the name of the game in government, which is in cahoots with the media to create crises where there aren't any. In that way, the media can sell more papers or magazines or time on TV and radio, and government BigShots can look official as they busily go about their business of saving us from the crisis de jour.

Drama can be the name of the game in business as well, but only if it adds to the business's self-interests: revenues and profits.

❖ **_Legitimized_** with statistics and surveys, no matter how skewed and poorly designed they are. I had a standing offer at one of my clients that I could take any survey or set of statistics and draw any conclusion that a BigShot wanted. In short, I offered to interpret, some would say _skew_ or _spin,_ the research to legitimize policy decisions or marketing objectives.

I'm reminded of another pithy saying attributed to Mark Twain: "If you read the newspapers you are misinformed; if you don't read the newspapers, you are uninformed."

The bottom line is simply this: a huge percentage of the "information" we use to make decisions—what to buy, who to elect, where to attend college, which company to invest in, and so on---actually shrinks our knowledge because it is so skewed and, therefore, misleading. Here are four examples that I feel are among the more egregious:

1. The price of gasoline is too high. In fact, gasoline costs less than bottled water and less in the United States than just about anywhere else in the world, about half as much as in many countries in Europe. Instead of griping about the cost, count your blessings and thank the oil companies for being so efficient.
2. The profits of oil companies are obscene: In fact, the profitability of oil companies, at around 8—10 percent of sales-- places them in the middle of all manufacturers, well

below Apple's at 24 percent, McDonald's at 20 percent, and so on.

3. Fuel efficiency standards—CAFÉ-- will save consumers big bucks. In fact, standards will force manufacturers to decrease the size and weight of cars and trucks by using stronger, lighter, more expensive materials, adding at least $3000 to sticker prices. The manufacturers don't care: If the standards are imposed equally on all, none will lose competitive advantage, market share, or profitability. In addition, the smaller, lighter cars will be less able to withstand a crash, so thousands more people will die on the roads.

4. Alternative sources of fuels such as ethanol and hydrogen, and alternative sources of electricity such as solar panels and windmills, will lead to energy independence…all primal BS that is addressed elsewhere in this book.

5. Republicans are conservatives who lack compassion and are against government regulations. In fact, conservatives donate more to charities as a percentage of their incomes than liberals, and encourage regulations, a.k.a. big government, as witnessed when Bush II added 90,000 federal employees during his tenure.

."The purpose of Newspeak…is to make all other modes of thought impossible." George Orwell.

"Get your facts first, and then you can distort them as much as you please." Mark Twain

CHAPTER 14: PAY FOR PERFORMANCE
   I Now Pronounce You Rich and Infamous….

We all know the fable of the fox that was let into the hen-house by the naïve farmer who thought the fox would protect the hens from other foxes, but instead enjoyed the easiest meal of its life. Now the fable is being repeated in countless boardrooms and executive suites. Yes, greedy CEOs hire foxy consultants to study compensation levels throughout the world and recommend pay and perks for the top dogs that are "competitive", a.k.a. exorbitant, and then justify their conclusions as "needed to attract top talent" such as themselves.

One result is that the consultant is rewarded exorbitantly for recommending exorbitant compensation for his client—how's that as an example of that incestuous arrangement called cronyism? -- and gasoline is poured on the fire of another vicious and self-serving cycle. Another result is that executive compensation is now more than 400 times—I've read some stats that put the number as high as 530 times-- that of the average employee, up from only 20 times in the 1960s, 42 times in the 1980s. The staggering spiral is sure to continue spiraling up as the foxes continue to inhabit the hen house. You pat my back, I'll pat yours has become standard procedure, and it's fueled by the greed that makes Midas look like a novice.

Perhaps the beginnings of runaway greed can be traced to financier Ivan F. Boesky when he told the 1985 graduating class at the University of California Berkeley School of Business Administration that "greed is healthy." (He didn't say for whom.) He was followed several years later when Michael Douglas said, in the movie Wall Street, that "greed is good". Those two pronouncements helped to transform greed from a despicable sin to an enviable virtue that is displayed in the business press almost every day. Unfortunately, the public seems to have become immune to such public selfishness.

The top dogs also hire consultants to evaluate the pay levels of the troops in the trenches, but not to justify higher pay. This little morale-busting ploy is to justify steady or lower compensation levels in the name of efficiency or productivity. In my experience, the consultants usually ask employees to write their job descriptions and then re-apply for the job that they already have, pissing everybody off big-time. Then they use complex formulae to establish compensation levels for various jobs, and they invariably call for the status quo or cuts, and then rank the firm as paying above average for its industry to prevent a mass exodus of the slaves and to attract more of the same ilk. The troops are supposed to be placated by all this. Raises are rare. The top guys make out like the bandits they are; the other guys make out like the peons they are.

Tom Peters, the co-author of that fabulously best-selling tome that came out to much fanfare in the mid nineteen-seventies, *In Search of Excellence,* said this about compensation: "Reward excellent failures; punish mediocre successes." If we take those words at face value—and I think it's unfair to do so--Tom would embrace Ken Lay and Jeffrey Skillings of Enron, the entire Regas clan at Adelphia, and the misguided folks who brought Westinghouse to its knees before executive chicanery became fashionable in the media. Excellent failures all. (An aside: I'm sure that Tom's purpose was to encourage risk-taking, not failing. His idea was OK; his choice of words not.)

At this point I wonder how "excellent" is defined in this context: the bigger, more spectacular the failure, the more headlines it attracts, the more excellent it is? Or maybe it means that the idea or whatever it was that failed seemed spectacularly good when first proposed and didn't make the grade for reasons that nobody could have seen. Such failures are deemed to be excellent simply because someone tried to make them work.

The debate over CEO pay has been wallowing around in the business press for decades, maybe longer. In its May/June, 1992, issue Harvard Business Review published rebuttals to an earlier article titled *Who Should set CEO Pay? The Press? Congress? Shareholders?* The authors of the article, two lawyers, argue that the real question is not, as the press insists," are executives paid too much?" Instead they ask: "Are shareholders getting their money's worth?" Rather than cut executive pay or bind it with government restrictions, as some politicians have urged, the authors suggest that corporations extend incentive-based compensation plans to all employees, thus establishing *pay for performance* at every level of the organization.

The rebutters note that—and I am paraphrasing—company performance cannot account for more than about five percent of the variation in CEO pay…I cannot conclude that there is a high correlation between CEO pay and company performance…the real issue is pay for performance…the starting point (to bringing pay in line with reality) should be truly independent boards of directors who truly advocate shareholder and not management interests… but that is impossible when ninety-eight percent of the board members in corporate America were handed their positions by the CEO or his/her handpicked nominations committee (think cronyism and rubber stamps).

 The issue is not paying for past performance but improving future performance (try to apply that to CEOs like the final four at

Westinghouse). And lastly, as a summary, the Harvard Business Review (HBR) notes that the polarized income in the United States represents a dangerous trend for a democratic society. Now remember that CEO pay when this was written in the 1960s was about 15 times the average in the company; now it is 400 to 600 times. This is progress? Don't the folks who wrote the articles in HBR deserve the title of BigShot Bullshitters? Doesn't HBR itself? And perhaps the broader question: Does HBR influence readers/managers in any way? How irrelevant is this pompous rag?

 "It's only in the wacky world of CEOs where you get severance for failing", said Nell Minow, editor of The Corporate Library. Wacky, yes, and even worse: morale-destroying, unethical, dishonest, distasteful and more.

Big business would do a lot to repair its reputation if it really meant it when it says it will Pay for Performance, and then adopt another axiom:

Payback for Non-Performance.

Don't hold your breath for that to happen. The fox is firmly embedded in the hen-house, and stockholders, those "most important" folks who are far too helpless to change a system of compensation that is so obviously stacked against them, can't do a thing about it.

I am absolutely outraged—and I realize that nobody gives a shit that I am-- at the unbalanced compensation policies that permeate big business and that are justified as "fair" by the very BigShots who benefit. I am equally outraged that I see no end in sight, and that stockholders and employees aren't revolting in horror at the inequities that threaten their economic health. And I am outraged that all of us concerned about the future of business and free enterprise aren't shouting about the obvious failures of Pay for Performance. My outrage flares almost out of control at the obvious fork-tongued pronouncements of BigShots who defend their escalating pay out of one side of their mouths and Managing for Stockholder Value and Employees are our Most Important Assets out of the other, perhaps the ultimate in duplicitous bullshit.

If you own stocks or are employed by a BigShot firm and aren't as outraged as I am, maybe you should ask yourself *why*?

And you might consider the "say-on-pay" movement, a modest beginning that will give shareholders an advisory vote on BigShots' compensation. According to one report, 40 percent of investors support the movement, and a growing number of companies are agreeing to establish an independent board. Perhaps it is the first step to capping BigShots' pay, but, pessimist that I am, I doubt it. The trend to huge raises unrelated to performance has the strengths of longevity, tradition, and cronyism.

A modest proposal for all stockholders: Start a movement for *two boards* at every company, one with the traditional makeup, the second composed of smaller stockholders with a record of success managing stable, smaller businesses. Then give each board equal power to influence all decisions, creating a system of checks and balances that just might either eliminate or soften excesses. And, if that's not enough, all members of both boards serve without pay, which I'm certain will force members to decide if their loyalties are to the firm or to their wallets.

I'm sure that many of you out there, especially those now on traditional boards, will say that two boards guarantee gridlock and that the business would stagnate; still others will say that healthy debate among reasonable people, a.k.a. dialectic, will lead to more rational, equitable, democratic decisions. I side with the latter group, and I'd love to see some forward-looking company take the lead…and offer my services to help.

***

PS: This just in as I write this in mid-2013: The highest-paid CEO in Western Pennsylvania, according to the Tribune Review of Sunday, June 2, is Brett Harvey of Consol Energy. During 2012 his total compensation rose three percent to$17.7 million while the company's profits dropped 39 percent and stock price dropped 16 percent.

John Surma of U.S. Steel was paid $11.1 million, up 9 percent from 2011, while the company lost $124 million and the stock slid 16 percent.

William Johnson at H.J. Heinz was paid a mere $16.2 million (down 13 percent from 2011) while the company's profit slid 7 percent and stock price rose 4 percent, well below the major financial indices.

GMI Ratings, which tracks executive pay, reported that John Hammergren, CEO and Chairman of McKesson, was awarded a lump sum retirement package worth $159 million, the largest ever. Trailing John is Rupert Murdoch, Chairman and CEO of News Corp., at $74 million. On the good news, bad news side, GMI also reported that the average value of the pensions of 54 percent of the companies in the Standard and Poor's index dropped from $11.5 million to just over $7.0 million. That heartening news was blunted by the explanation for the drop: several CEOs with large pensions are retiring, not corporate restraint.

CHAPTER 15: LEGAL VS. ETHICAL
   The Distinction That Stinks ...

"Ethics stays in the prefaces of the average business science book." Peter Drucker

My corollary: *"Who the hell says business is a science?"*

Whenever I doubt the truth of Goethe's words, *"When an idea is wanting, a word can always be found to take its place",* I read a short folio published by a huge manufacturer titled *Code of Business Ethics and Conduct.* It's a sanctimonious pile of bull, a.k.a. words that are totally unrelated to actions.

A small diversion: *Ethics* as an idea isn't wanting, of course, and I wish there was more of it everywhere in our society, particularly in government, business, and the legal "profession", for which I and millions of other Americans hold little or no respect. That said, I see and experience a great deal of ethics in many of the executive suites I visit and damn little of it in others. I see almost none of it at the top in the company that authored *The Code* that I referred to above, which I assure you is difficult for me to say since so many of my good friends either work there or did at one time in their careers.

I do, however, hear a steady stream of lip service. I asked a friend who is a self-styled ethicist and owns a small engineering firm if, during the course of his 35-year career, he had ever come across a firm or a BigShot or two that he considered ethical. His reply: "Excepting my own firm the answer is a flat-out no. The owners and managers of the several firms I worked for before becoming my own boss would do anything to line their pockets, no matter who it hurt. And my clients were and are cut from the same cloth;

most would stretch the terms of our contracts if they thought for a minute that they would benefit economically."

I interrupted: "I am convinced that the vast majority of businesspersons are ethical; I've been in business for 40 years based totally on verbal agreements, not even handshakes. Neither I nor my clients ever asked for a written contract. I was cheated only twice, both times for small sums." "You were very fortunate" he replied, "perhaps because you chose your clients more carefully."

*   *   *

"Ethics" is also one of the many words that is tough to define simply because each of us holds our own definition in our heads and hearts. Mine is perhaps too simplistic but it works for me: To never hurt another person physically, fiscally, or emotionally. Perhaps I stole that from the medical profession's Hippocratic Oath to first, do no harm. The other side of that coin, the proactive and positive side, is to help people who are in physical, fiscal, or emotional need or pain whenever I can.

My definition is in line with Albert Schweitzer's: "A man is ethical only when life, as such, is sacred to him, that of plants and animals as well as that of his fellowman, and when he devotes himself helpfully to all life that is in need of help."

A friend defines ethics a bit differently: equal and large doses of honesty, respect, responsibility, fairness, and compassion. He is writing a book that dedicates a chapter to each of these attributes: their precise definitions, historical examples of use and misuse, and why and how BigShots could and should embrace them.

I'm sure I've violated my definition during my long and fruitful life, but almost never intentionally. I could tell you tales of people who have violated that definition and hurt me, especially fiscally and emotionally, but this is not a trial.

Back to *The Code*. Its very first sentence mixes and confuses ethics, morality, and laws "…our policy is to comply with all laws…and to conduct our affairs with the highest moral, legal, and ethical standards." *The Code* continues: "Even where the law does not apply, applicable standards of ethics and morality relate to our activities and require the same diligence and attention to good conduct and citizenship."

Two points: If surveys can be believed, a whopping 77 percent of American adults don't trust lawyers to tell the truth, a simple act when compared to the broader concept of ethics. Many of the folks I call friends think of lawyers as self-serving blood suckers out to hurt anybody fiscally and emotionally if doing so means they will be paid outlandishly high fees. One friend is convinced that lawyers are the root cause of our most egregious problems of trust and morality, and seriously hinder our economic and social progress. Another is convinced that the one common denominator in all lapses of ethics is the law, or, more explicitly, a greedy lawyer. Still another friend, trained as a lawyer, quit his lucrative partnership in a small firm because he lost respect for a profession that was once so esteemed. He wanted to "rejoin humanity".

Mixing 'the law' with ethics and morality is a major contradiction. And "Even where the law does not apply…" places the law above ethics and morality, exactly where it shouldn't be. A friend and policy wonk categorizes ethics, morality, and good behavior in three levels of ascending importance. On the bottom is the law, which applies to all of us,

supposedly in equal doses—try not to laugh at that blatant bull--
and is enforceable in the sense that defined infractions are
punishable in defined ways. In the middle is ethics, the unwritten
codes of behavior that are held by individuals that are not specified
by the law and which are not enforceable. And on the top is
morality, the code of behavior that applies to all of us collectively
as a civil society, again unwritten and unenforceable.

So the managers who say, "I don't care if it's ethical. Is it legal?"
are merely following the directive from the BigShots, which of
course is the Nuremberg Defense. For you who are not familiar
with the Nuremberg Defense, it was the rationale for German
officers after WW II during the Nuremberg trials for killing
millions of Jews and others: "I was merely following orders."

The contradictions in *The Code* between words and actions
continue. A few examples: "Employees shall not request or accept
monetary loans or personal services from suppliers…" I, a
supplier, loaned ten thousand dollars to an employee of the firm as
a down payment on his house that he couldn't scrape up. To his
credit, the employee paid me back as planned, which of course
didn't erase his, and my, violation of *The Code.*

A bigger violation: The CEO of this same firm "asked" suppliers
to help build his retirement home in the nearby mountains. He--the
CEO—never paid back a dime that I know of after checking with
several of the suppliers. But I'll bet that the suppliers padded their
next bills, committing their own ethical transgressions in the name
of fiscal survival. Can you blame them?

The Code continues: "Employees may not accept gifts or
gratuities…with the exception of advertising novelties of a
nominal value marked with the donor's company name." What a

pile of bullshit that is! I lost count years ago of the many golf games, fancy dinners, tickets to shows and so on that I gave my clients and their spouses, and that they accepted without a second thought. My competitors did the same. And I will never forget a client of mine who, after accepting a posh and expensive lunch, asked me to shop with him for a new set of tableware for his wife. As we strolled through the boutique, he pointed to one particularly attractive and expensive set and remarked several times how much his wife would enjoy it. I of course got the not-so-subtle hint and …never talked to or worked with him again; I was always "too busy". Surprised?

Don't be: it was one of my best business decisions. He was violating his firm's code of ethics, and I could easily have enabled him to do so. But…was it illegal? Only if he failed to report the gift as income on his next tax return. I of course would have reported it as expense on mine, so he would have been vulnerable to the IRS' cross-checking and could very well have been caught for evasion. When I told this story to other clients in the same firm, I was rewarded with a plethora of new assignments.

In truth, we as a society have made *ethical* and *legal* synonyms, just as we have made *unethical* and *illegal* synonyms, and the reason is clear in my mind: it's simpler. Our laws are spelled out in huge volumes found in countless public and private libraries, and they—the laws-- are interpreted every day by judges who are almost always lawyers themselves, and are supposedly fair and unbiased. (You who have ever been in court can stop laughing now.)

The laws and interpretations are written to avoid ambiguities, so they are, in theory, clear. They aren't totally, of course; if they were, we wouldn't need so many lawyers and judges to continuously interpret them. As further proof that we have meshed ethical and legal, many firms have appointed a Compliance Officer to whom employees can ask questions about ethical behavior and report ethical misconduct; the officers are usually in the legal department.

On the other hand, *ethics* is spelled out by the Bible, the Koran, and similar books published by countless religions. The books are written in extremely vague and abstract terms that are often contradictory, and therefore have been interpreted continuously by theologians based on their personal biases and beliefs. In addition, their interpretations are typically not written; they're spoken in sermons and homilies, so they are not accessible to the public.

The bottom line is, simply, that the law is theoretically more concrete and, therefore, its interpretation easier; you and I can walk into the myriad law offices so endemic in our culture, and, for a fee, get an interpretation. In addition, the law spells out immediate and visible punishments for various levels of breaches, while the churches do not. An afterlife in Hell is not by any stretch either immediate or visible.

Perhaps our confusion about *ethical* and *legal* is best explained by this true story told to me by a friend who was there. The solution to a major scandal in a department of the Federal Government was supposedly solved in a way that was typically bureaucratic: A class was thrown together at the national level and all appropriate employees were forced to attend and be trained in ethics. The young lady who taught the class pointed to examples of practices that didn't comply with regulations, laws, or policies. There was no attempt to establish any moral link to ethics. When one attendee asked if everything that is legal is ethical, the teacher stumbled and mumbled, demonstrating nicely that she had never thought of the connection, and neither had her superiors. She did, however, make sure that all attendees signed the attendance sheet to certify that she had done her job.

The confusion between *legal* and *ethical,* and the emphasis on *legal,* is demonstrated further in *The Code*: The words *ethics* and *morality* appear exactly six times (and not once after page two) in its 27 pages; the word *legal* and its variations appear 34 times. In addition, one chapter is entitled *Illegal Payments;* no chapter title mentions ethics. It's so easy to transfer our responsibilities for ethics to the lawyers, who gladly accept the extra work.

However, many contradictions about his sordid behavior remain in limbo, and
I could go on and on with tales of unethical behavior by BigShots at all levels, but …

Please read APPENDIX A for more on this very important and intriguing topic.

CHAPTER 16: MANAGING FOR SHAREHOLDER VALUE
The Love of Money...

The biggest pile of bullshit since the Tulip Mania of the 1600s is this from the mouths of BigShots: "We all benefit equally from higher stock prices." Nothing could be further from the truth, which is, simply, that BigShots win big, and LittleShots win little or, if they're very little, not at all.

The craziest part of managing for shareholder value—MSV—is that many of the little guys believe that it's good for them, proving that age-old maxim that repeating anything, no matter how far-fetched, often enough creates "truth". The little guys who fall for the BigShots' bull must be mathematical and financial idiots to believe in the universal benefits of MSV, or they are so damned loyal to or intimidated by BigShots that they can't think straight.

Many business persons think that MSV is new, a product of modern capitalism. In fact, MSV is centuries old. The capitalist corporation was born at least as far back as the early 1600s, when royalty in the major trading nations—Holland, England, and Spain—realized their coffers weren't big enough to finance the exploration and expansion of trade that they envisioned. (Bigger is better and diversify or die were powerful mantras even back then.) So they granted charters to companies for specific purposes and durations, and the companies sold shares in their ventures to the public. The companies were the precursors of the modern corporation, and trading of their shares the precursors of the modern stock exchanges.

The United States was settled by one such corporation, the Massachusetts Bay Company, which was granted its charter in 1628 by England's King Charles I. The company expanded the government's power through colonization, annexing resources (including slave labor), and creating markets in which to sell goods. Nation-building and capitalism grew in lockstep.

The corporation soon became the financial mechanism that built the modern world, largely because its charter excused owners/investors from personal responsibility for their actions, no matter how devious. This single change in thinking and in the legal system that backed it liberated creativity and risk-taking, which in turn catapulted a significant portion of humanity out of poverty and another, smaller portion into poverty, as we all know; there are no panaceas, also known as no free lunches.

It also created a machine that could be soulless that was built too often on greed and arrogance—a machine that made fraud very attractive for those in control. The first corporations were plagued by fraud and other scandals, as unscrupulous jobbers, the precursors to today's stockbrokers, sold shares in fake companies to naïve or greedy investors looking for a quick fortune. Recent examples include the dot-com mania of the 1990s and the real estate boom of the early 2000s. Both were examples of what Alan Greenspan, the former Chairman of the Federal Reserve, called "irrational exuberance".
 Both turned to busts in only a few short years, and the real estate bust has turned into a "crisis" that, supposedly, threatened the stability of the entire world's economy. It did roil the world's stock and currency markets. And, as I write this in 2013, a new bust is in the works as Obama loosens credit as the economy recovers, which is another sordid example of total, self-serving bullshit to the millions of Americans still unemployed.

Over the centuries, protection of shareholders' assets became the sole or primary mandate of top management. The courts agreed, and ruled in case after case in favor of the corporation and against society, largely employees, consumers, communities, and the environment. Thus, MSV became a legal mandate, literally preventing managers from being morally and socially responsible even if they wanted to be. Or, to turn that thought around, MSV literally forces managers to behave immorally and irresponsibly in some circumstances—not all, by any stretch-- in order to protect shareholders.

I want to point out here that I am fully aware that many employees of corporations and limited partnerships at every level are totally convinced that managing for stockholder value is the only moral and responsible mantra for management. Their rationale is—and I know that I am simplifying here-- that the creation of wealth is good for everyone in society, not just for investors. They cite that old saw that a rising tide lifts all boats. Stated another way, if each corporation pursues its own self-interest, the result will be positive for all. That's true up to the point where the tide is dropping because of the perverse, short-term decisions that MSV often dictates. Then MSV becomes classic...

Bullshit.

A compromise between MSV and broader, more charitable purposes is possible, as demonstrated by any number of profitable corporations that also respect society: Whole Foods, Mine Safety Appliances, H.J. Heinz, McKesson and a raft of smaller firms come immediately to mind. Finding this middle ground requires that managers forget what they learned in business school—that the corporation is *solely* a machine for making money—and learn that the corporation is *partly for making money and partly for contributing to the human community.*

Here's another viewpoint: "Contrary to business school doctrine, maximizing shareholder wealth, or profit maximization, has not been the driving force or primary objective throughout the history of visionary companies (those formed before 1950 and still the premier institution in their industries). Visionary companies pursue a cluster of objectives, of which making money is only one—and not necessarily the primary one. Yes, they seek profits, but they're equally concerned by a core ideology—core values and a sense of purpose beyond just making money. Yet, paradoxically, the visionary companies make more money than the more purely profit-driven comparison companies." (From *Built to Last: Successful Habits of Visionary Companies,* by James C. Collins and Jerry I. Porres.)

To those of you who would like to read more on this important topic, I recommend *The Fifth Discipline* by Peter Senge, *Cause for Success* by Christine Arena, the aforementioned *Built to Last, Good Company,* by Laura Blasi et al, and *The Power of Dignity* by Pete Geissler.

CHAPTER 17: MY PERSONAL LIFE IS MINE
   You Can Fool Most of the People ...

I consulted for many years with the president of a manufacturer with annual sales of around ten billion dollars, and I always thought of him as one of the more honest and decent BigShots I had ever met. Then, for reasons I'll never know, he, married to a woman of great charm and wisdom, allegedly (we'll never know for sure, but the perception of truth can serve as truth) started an affair with a mid-level employee who was married to another employee of the same firm. And, in another example of the arrogance of BigShots, he and she made very little effort to hide their alleged affair, and they were seen together at lunches and out-of-town meetings.

The BigShot thought that nobody would care or notice, proving that stupidity in the form of naivete can cut through the highest IQs when lust, whether sexual or financial, enters the picture. He, the BigShot, then took stupidity and cronyism to an art form and promoted his apparent mistress to an executive position despite her apparent lack of qualifications and experience. The rumor mill went wild and morale went into the toilet, along with productivity.

When I approached this BigShot and told him what was happening to his company, career, and reputation, he told me that his personal life was nobody's business but his own.

Bullshit. Not so. Every BigShot's public and personal lives are one and the same, and the bigger the BigShot the more that is true. The notion that public behavior is different than private behavior has been debunked many times in recent years: Gary Hart and Diana Rice, Bill Clinton and Monica Lewinski, the governor and lieutenant governor of New York, Roger Clemens and Tiger

Woods and their many alleged affairs, and, in business, the entire family that ran Adelphia into the ground.

Regardless, my BigShot friend continued on his unaware way, the firm's productivity and morale continued to slide, and he made a series of perverse decisions that seriously eroded his credibility as an ethical, forthright man who could be trusted to lead a large organization. And, I want to point out here once again that without trust human relations of any sort or a moral society are impossible.

The board finally caught on to what was happening to the company and fired BigShot. Too late. The company slid into bankruptcy and was sold in pieces to several other firms, and the pieces are thriving under more honest and competent management.

The last time I saw BigShot he told me that he still couldn't understand what had happened to his company and career. And, by the way, his mistress went home to hubby.

CHAPTER 18: MBAs AND LAWYERS KNOW BEST
   Take a Look at DC ...

I'm reminded at this point of Jean-Jacques Rousseau, the French philosopher who lived from 1712-1778. He wrote in his *Social Contract*: "Wise men, if they try to speak their language to the common herd instead of its own, cannot possibly make themselves understood. There are a thousand kinds of ideas which it is impossible to translate into common language."

Rousseau is correct. I often hear people at social events, usually by folks who have reinforced their opinions with a few drinks, and talking heads on TV and radio, usually by self-proclaimed pundits with axes to grind, expound on the stupidity of Bush II, our first MBA President.

Nobody with an IQ over 10 could argue that Bush II didn't make a raft of bad decisions. The most egregious was, of course, the Iraq war and his arrogant display on an aircraft carrier soon after the war started, when, dressed in military garb, he told us that the worst of the fighting was over. As far as I can tell, Bush made only one decision that could be dubbed "good". At least for the first seven years of his disgraceful stay in the oval office, he meddled minimally with our economy, and we have enjoyed some pretty prosperous years as the free market did its thing. So his best decision was to do little or nothing.

I'd like to think that he made another good decision, also based on doing nothing. He refused to sign the Kyoto Treaty. But, along the way he wavered and talked about reversing himself and kissing the asses of millions in our naïve population (read "voters") who believe the bullshit of the global warming freaks, including and especially Al Gore. Yes, man-made global warming is the biggest hoax, a.k.a. bullshit, since the tulip mania of the 1600s, and falling for it will cost our country trillions, just what our enemies want.

Anyway, I, often, and sometimes for the fun of pricking the bubbles of those folks who, in a moment of intellectual arrogance, are so sure that Bush is stupid, counter with a simple question: If Bush is so stupid, why did he win two elections that he was supposed to lose by wide margins? (By the way, if you haven't noticed by reading the above, I decidedly am *not* a Bush supporter.)

That seemingly simple query ... if Bush is so stupid ... invariably puzzles the countless Bush haters that I know, and I am greeted with either blank stares or stutters.

The contradiction here is that smart people often can't communicate with those who aren't so smart, and less-smart people can. Ergo, Bush is not as smart as Gore and Kerry in some ways, but infinitely smarter in others.

I'm fond of telling this story on myself, a person who is reputed—please note that reputed is not at all related to reality, much as I'd like it to be-- to be smart. When Gore was nominated for the presidency, I bet several friends the best dinners in Pittsburgh that he, Gore, would win by 100 electoral votes. I wrongly reasoned—and defied my own warnings about the uselessness and inaccuracies of predictions--that anyone even remotely connected to the greatest economic and stock market boom in history would walk away with all the marbles.

Gore, to my knowledge, never mentioned his involvement. I can only surmise that he and his advisers decided to distance him from the Clinton sex and other scandals, but, in doing so, they distanced him from the booms.

Being a slow learner, I made the same bet with the same people when Kerry was nominated, erroneously reasoning again that Bush's popularity was so low that he'd be swept out of office by even the weakest opposition. But Kerry's campaign was centered on "I'm not Bush", a message devoid of any useful ideas or ideals that would appeal to anybody looking to vote *for* a candidate, not *against* one.

I decided early in my career to get an MBA, not because I wanted to be smarter than I already was, but because folks with MBAs were, and still are, paid more money than those who hold merely an undergraduate degree. Some people cite that one disputable fact as proof that MBAs make better decisions. Somehow, the cause/effect escapes me, probably because I know too many MBAs who can't think their way into or out of the outhouse. As an aside, I wrote several MBA and PhD theses for candidates who couldn't, which f course is against all the ethical principles of every university worth the paper its diplomas are printed on.

So I enrolled at a local, mildly prestigious university, and soon quit. I became thoroughly disillusioned and disgusted when one economics professor openly espoused communism when I thought we were there to learn about free enterprise and democracy. Another professor professed emphatically that every business problem or issue could be solved with mathematics—that mathematics is the way to better decisions. Yet, time after time, problem after problem, he couldn't demonstrate his own premise by completing his calculations, surely because his premise is totally wrong and wrong-headed, and he wouldn't or couldn't admit it.

And I know executives with MBAs who can't think in what I would call logical or coherent ways. Many of them hire me to help them, and the brighter ones admit that I am most useful to them when I do so, not when I write a gangbuster speech or strategic plan. That's not unusual when you consider that writers in general are typically ranked among the smartest; if they weren't, why are they popular after-dinner speakers and why do universities insist on "publish or perish"? (For more on the omniscience of writers, please read *Genius*, by Harold Bloom, and be rewarded with mind-popping insights.)

I cannot resist a word about Einstein, and why his name is embedded in our language as a synonym for intelligence. Yes, he was a physicist of great insight; he was also a fine writer, able to express his complex theories in ways so that even the President of the United States could understand their implications.

If Gore and Kerry could have pulled that off in 2000 and 2004, perhaps the world would be a different place. Then again, given our pitiful record of projections, how would we know?

CHAPTER 19: SOCIAL RESPONSIBILITY
  When Pigs Fly ...

As I've said earlier, I've thought for years that the Harvard
Business Review (HBR) leads the way in business bull, and an
article titled *Do Well by Doing Good? Don't Count on it* helps to
confirm it. The authors, both academicians, condense a 35-year
study that tries to equate doing well, which is clearly defined as
raising profits and shareholder value (see above for my strong
feelings about that flavor of bull) with doing good, which is
loosely defined as contributions to charities and even more loosely
as community projects, whatever they are.

One conclusion by the authors stands out: "Corporate misdeeds are
costly to companies—if people find out." I translate that gem to
mean that misdeeds are OK if nobody knows about them. Digging
further, I think it means that HBR and that venerable institution
that supports it, Harvard University, sanctions covert misdeeds
even though I know deep down that they don't. Nevertheless, I
think that their words express a total lack of ethics that perhaps is
another of the many sins that Harvard and other business schools
have perpetrated on the world, particularly and especially
managing for profits and shareholder value. As I've already made
clear, I am a firm believer in free enterprise and the need for profits
to feed it. I just think that too many social and criminal misdeeds
are committed pursuing that mantra and some balance is needed.

The authors dig a deeper hole: "Anecdotal evidence about recent
scandals highlights just how grave the consequences of
wrongdoing can be for companies and their executives, but it's
difficult to estimate the likelihood of being found out."

Tell me: what the hell do corporate misdeeds--which in this context means accounting manipulations or cooking the books to raise earnings for the short term while sacrificing the long term-- have to do with social responsibility? Aren't the authors off on a wild excursion?

Another conclusion: "Doing good is unlikely to cost shareholders. The proof: only two percent of the studies reviewed shows that those who dedicate corporate resources to social performance … impose a direct cost to shareholders. Companies can do good *and* do well, even if they don't do well by doing good."

I had to read that twisted sentence three times to translate: Companies that are socially responsible might also increase shareholder value, but companies cannot expect that being socially responsible will increase shareholder value. There is no cause and effect here.

So, given that too many of today's BigShots cling to that awful mantra of managing for shareholder value, why be socially responsible? The authors have an answer: "None of this is to suggest that companies should not engage in activities that generate social good. However they should not expect to be handsomely rewarded. Socially responsible behavior may not cost you (sic) financially, but if the goal is return on investment, there are many other ways to spend money that can deliver a greater payoff." My heavens, did the authors need to tell their readers, BigShots all, that investing in new computers, say, pays off, a.k.a. increases profits, bigger than, say, sponsoring an opera company?

The article closes: "Doing good may be its own reward." I interpret that to mean that social responsibility allows managers to get a good night's sleep, or, as the authors point out, to avoid running afoul of regulators and activists and its distracting hassles.

Perhaps you'll be surprised to know that I tend to defend business, and I will here: Every one of the hundred or so businesspeople I know contributes to society in some way, as I do. I don't think that they consider their contributions to be anything more than their responsibility to the society that got them where they are. In other words, they think of their contributions as thank you notes. I don't know Warren Buffet or Bill Gates, but I'd bet that they fall into that bailiwick. By the way, these same businesspeople pay taxes, some would say a disproportionately high or low share depending on their political leanings, that can also be thought of as support of, or payback to, society.

I think that the well-meaning folks at Harvard are spewing more bull with their study. And I think that the charlatans who have raped companies for their own gain, and, I hope, can't get a good night's rest or a peaceful dream, should study businessmen who reap the rewards of social responsibility.

I wish that all BigShots at every level and in every sort of organization could read this from *Cause for Success*: "The less credence a company gives to the social and environmental inequities surrounding it, particularly those inequities that its actions help to perpetuate, the less meaningful and invincible it tends to be. Inversely, the more a company operates with regard to the collective interest, the more it does something to improve people's lives and to solve society's problems, the more indispensable and sustainable it ultimately becomes. *Cause for Success* shows that positive correlations exist between a company's wider sense of purpose and its health, its value, and its ability to endure."

101

By the way, *sustainable* in this context means that the business is managed to stay in business, not fold under the weight of greed and arrogance, as did such firms as Enron and Westinghouse.

CHAPTER 20: THE BUSINESS OF SPORTS
Contract? What Contract?

The list of coaches at universities and professional teams who sign long-term and lucrative contracts while insisting how happy they are and vowing to stay on the job until retirement, then defecting for a better offer, is long and perhaps the apex of bull in this sports-crazed America. While I think that the coaches are unethical liars, I also think the universities and team owners are equally slimy; they are enablers in the worst way.

Why worst? Because universities pompously set themselves up as the arbiters of ethics, of intellectual honesty, and their PR has worked well. Professors, for example, are trusted to tell the truth by seventy-five percent of adult Americans. As trusted arbiters, professors are the role models for their students. In fact, they and administrators are pinnacles of hypocrisy.

I want to point out here that I taught for years at a mid-size university whose motto toys with "mind, body, and spirit", noble thoughts all. I honestly think that the good folks who manage and teach at this institution live by their motto, and I honestly think that one reason they can and do so is simply that they have not fallen into the trap of big-time sports, or of big-time university, for that matter. I think that big-time sports have the same power to corrupt, i.e. encourage unethical behavior to make a buck, as big-time business or politics. And I am convinced that as big-time grows to bigger-time (an inevitable transition in a society that thinks, oh so wrongly, that bigger is better and the only viable options are to either grow or die) corruption becomes increasingly more attractive. I'm reminded of that old saying attributed to Lord Acton (1834-1902) that power tends to corrupt, and absolute power corrupts absolutely. It was enhanced and clarified by Lincoln

Steffens, who noted that power is what men seek, and any group that gets it will abuse it.

Recent examples abound and have been well-publicized, so I won't add to the din.

To be sure, other coaches and owners honor their contracts and believe in long-term stability. Basketball coach Mike Krzyewski— Coach K-- at Duke comes immediately to mind; he is finishing more than 30 successful and admirable years despite being lured with big bucks by several NBA franchises.

The owners of the Pittsburgh Steelers fall into the same basket; they carefully select their coaches and sign them to long-term contracts and the coaches honor them. The results are in the stats: The Steelers have had three head coaches since 1969, and the third is still on the job as I write this. The team has won more games and championships, including six Super Bowls, than any other in the NFL. The owners and coaches deliver exciting football played by championship contenders almost every season, and the fans show their appreciation by filling the stadium for every game.

The Pittsburgh Pirates, on the other hand, haven't learned a thing from their neighbors, the Steelers. The owners, who promised a contender if only the taxpayers would pay for a new stadium, change managers every few years—I cannot count the number of managers the team has hired during the past 30 years. The revolving door is a vain and idiotic attempt to find that silver bullet without paying for talent on the field. The Pirates are the perfect example of managing for profits by cutting employee costs, then barely making any profit because they offer a lousy product in a fancy package.

I often wonder how long the owners think that they can continue this rip-off of the public. Big Shots just traded two of the team's best players for a scraggly few unknowns and wannabes, I'm sure reducing payrolls to fatten profits for the short term, a sure-fire way to guarantee failure. Nevertheless, the trades are justified as "best for the long-term success of the team."

By the way, I live only a few minutes' walk to the Pirates' stadium, and I absolutely refuse to attend a game. I cannot abide multiplying the insult of politicians ripping me off for the money to build a stadium by the extreme insult of BigShots ripping me off to watch bad baseball. When the Pirates call me to ask that I buy season tickets and I refuse and they ask why, I tell them that I don't buy a Yugo car either. I doubt that they understand the analogy. A prominent sports writer in this town told me that I should support the Pirates if I want a better team. I told him that he has it backwards, that the owners won't pay for and field a better team until they start to lose money. In my mind, that's a basic precept of marketing.

Maybe, just maybe, the tide has turned: The Pirates hired a manager and awarded him a long-term contract after one exciting but losing 2012 season, and the team has the second-best record in baseball as I write this, in July 2013. I'd love to admit that I was wrong about the short-term, self-serving BigShots who own and run the team, but won't until the end of the 2014 season.

Universities justify their huge sports programs by avowing that sports are part of a well-rounded education that builds character, strong values, and a greater sense of ethics. Yet, as Rushmore Kidder reports in his book, *How Good People Make Tough Choices*: "Intercollegiate sports, as currently played on the competitive, televised, and money-sodden fields of many of today's campuses, apparently does just the reverse. It takes whatever capacity for moral reasoning the athletes bring with them and corrodes it slowly away as the seasons pass."

I'm reminded of Peter Drucker's comment that when an institution loses its focus on its primary goal, it is on the road to oblivion. Perhaps universities and professional sports might heed the warning.

They might also consider that they too often live, clearly and vividly, the definition of bull that I love so much—the disconnect between words and actions. Examples abound, but one stands out. Early in 2008, the owner of a professional football team announced that he was getting out of the business of rehabilitating the ten players on his ream who had been arrested during the previous fourteen months. Included among the ten was a wide receiver who had been arrested five times. The owner stated clearly that this player's conduct can no longer be tolerated, echoing a local judge who called the player a one-man crime wave.

Nevertheless, and in a remarkable and shameful display of self-interest overcoming any sense of honesty and ethics, the owner gave the player one more chance and a two-year contract worth multi-millions just four months after he was released by the team. The unstated reason: injuries to two other players, requiring a quick fix despite the obvious bull shit—at least to me, but I gotta wonder about the team's fans.

CHAPTER 21: STATISTICS
Lies, damn Lies, and Statistics ...

Statistical treatment to prove causal relationships can be superstition and witchcraft.

The secret language of statistics, so appealing in our fact-seeking culture, is used to sensationalize, distort, confuse, inflate, and over-simplify so many issues and by so many corporate and government bull shitters that it may be the most endemic form of bull of all, **even exceeding words**.

Here are a few ways it's done, complete with examples. First, samples with built-in biases. I told one client that I can prove anything if given a set of statistics, and I did on several occasions. Probably the most glaring was my proving, in the mid to late 1970s, that the world would run out of oil by 2000, which I addressed earlier but feel compelled to expand. It was easy: I just extended the historical trend lines of consumption and discoveries of new oil and, Voila! we're out of oil. Of course I neglected to factor in the effect of price on the law of supply and demand, and as prices increased so did the amount of recoverable oil. But the big neglected factor was my bias: I wanted to prove beyond a shadow of statistical doubt that nuclear plants are the solution to everybody's energy crises.

BTW, "energy crisis" is bullshit in itself. What's the problem? Availability? Not in the US, where we can fill our tanks and plug in our TVs and computers and be instantly gratified. Price? Not here. Gasoline here is less than half the price of gasoline in places like Europe and Asia. Quality? No problem. Imports of oil from our enemies in the Middle East? We now import less that 20 percent of our needs from those countries that are supposedly gouging us, and I think that we should thank instead of demonize them. High profits of oil producers? BIG, populist bullshit perpetrated by our politicians and media; the profitability of oil producers doesn't even rise to the median of all manufacturers. So tell me, what crisis? Please, don't tell me that we will soon "run out"; we've already seen the BS in that scare tactic.

Second, the truncated, gee-whiz, souped-up graph, a favorite in annual reports and of Al Gore in his misguided attempt to prove that humans are causing the globe to warm, or, more recently, the climate to change. All you need to do is compress a line graph sideways to show that trends are moving faster—as Gore did with his graph depicting accumulation of greenhouse gases and as countless annual reports do to show growth of revenues and profits, but never losses. You can do the opposite by opening the graph horizontally and lines will be flatter and the trend appears to be slower or less severe.

Third, the well-tempered "average". I can report that the average household income in my neighborhood is more than $100,000/ year—which I would do if I wanted to sell to persons with a high sense of snobbery-- or less than $30,000, which I would do if I were arguing against an increase in taxes or bus fares. Here's how I can arrive at whatever figure that suits my purpose: One of my 50 neighbors enjoys an annual income of more than one million dollars, the rest of us less than fifty thousand. More than half of them are retired and live on less than thirty thousand. Adding everyone's income and dividing by 50 arrives at an average of more than $100,000, creating a misleading mean. The smaller $30,000 is a median that half of us live below and half above. Which is the more realistic picture?

Fourth, assumptions that ignore history. A favorite of mine is the comparisons of today's prices with those of, say, the halcyon fifties. They make it seem that we now are burdened with huge prices when we aren't. Let's take an extreme but realistic example. Back in the mid 1970s we were paying about 25 cents for a gallon of gas and we were shouting obscenities at OPEC and each other. Today we are paying about four dollars a gallon, 16 times as much. Sounds awful until you understand that you are probably earning 16 times or more as much, which makes gas a bargain that has actually declined in price relative to the purchasing power of the dollar.

I don't know about you, but when I review my earnings history the numbers from the sixties and seventies are, in a word, quaint. Yet I lived on them very comfortably. BTW, in the seventies you could buy a car for around $2000. Today, you can't buy even a basic car for much less than $20,000, and $30,000 for a model that you'd drive would be closer to reality.

Going further back in time, that basket of groceries that you just bought for $100 cost a mere $2 in 1914, 50 times less. You can bet that average incomes were at least 50 times less as well; I say "at least" because increases in productivity have raised incomes faster than increases in inflation during the past century, one reason for our enviable standard of living.

The moral is to not wring your hands over today's "high prices". Most aren't, and some are way lower. Compare the real cost of your TV and telephone and computer and you'll see what I mean.

However, statistics can be useful if applied truthfully. One example: statistics were the critical tool during WW II that led to a large increase in the number of U-Boats sunk by the British Navy.

They—statistics—suggested new settings for depth charges, and that large convoys were less susceptible to attacks than small convoys.

On the other side of the war coin, the statistics used by Robert McNamara to run the Vietnam war were so distorted that they actually helped to create that deadly fiasco. They emphasized numbers such as body counts, which were grossly exaggerated, costs, and efficiency, and basically ignored human intuition. But the big problem was with McNamara and the other whiz kids: Their huge egos could not allow them to admit failure, enabling the same errors to be repeated over and over, which fit perfectly the popular definition of "crazy": doing something over and over and expecting a different result.

.

CHAPTER 22: INCONSISTENCIES AND CONTRADICTIONS
  Good, Bad, or Indifferent…

Consistency in words and actions is both a sin and a virtue: a sin when change is necessary, a virtue when stability and clarity of purpose are needed to meet specific purposes or goals.

Many of our most revered thinkers recognized and wrote about this apparent paradox. Perhaps the most famous was Ralph Waldo Emerson (1803—1862), who said: "A foolish consistency is the hobgoblin of little minds, adored by little statesmen and philosophers and divines. With consistency, a great soul simply has nothing to do."

Unfortunately, "foolish" is often omitted by those fools who quote him to prove that consistency is always bad, and they neglect to point out that "hobgoblin", an archaic term, means "cause of annoyance". Emerson was annoyed by consistency when inconsistency makes sense. He preferred flexibility.

 James Russell Lowell (1819—1891), an American poet and diplomat, favored inconsistency when he wrote that, "The foolish and the dead never change their opinions." Centuries earlier, Joseph Addison (1672—1719), an English essayist and co-founder of *The Spectator* magazine, favored consistency when he wrote that "Nothing that isn't a real crime makes a man appear so contemptible and little in the eyes of the world as inconsistency."

Regardless, the worlds of business and government are so full of bull that inconsistencies and contradictions—the gaping disconnects between words and actions or words and other words—are plentiful, and, I think, confusing.

Examples: Managing for shareholder value or for maximizing profits still seems to be the dominant mantra of companies and business schools. Yet the evidence is compelling to anyone who can read that managing for core values such as truth and integrity is more profitable and helps assure the continuity of the firm. Tell me, what is worse for shareholders than going out of business?

BigShots claim incessantly in speeches and in print that their employees and, at times, their customers, are their most important assets. Then they downsize or rightsize the firm and disrupt or destroy countless lives, often without good reason. And they drop long-standing customers because they can reap higher returns in other markets. Loyalty be damned.

BigShots claim to be "strategically oriented"…then make decisions that are obviously short-term fixes that actually hurt the firm over the longer term. They cut the advertising/PR and sales budgets during a downturn, exactly when those budgets should be increased if they're at all interested in grabbing a bigger share of their markets, as they always say they are. Big shots espouse pay for performance…then justify the outrageous compensation they and their cronies are given when their performance is lackluster or worse. .

BigShots to a person are proud of their individuality, their abilities to think on their own, to take charge of their firms … then they jump on the latest mantra that is usually endorsed by an outside consultant or another BigShot. BigShots talk about their commitment to their home base … then move their headquarters or the entire firm to another city. They say "we are not for sale" to squelch rumors that say otherwise … then sell or merge in order to raise the price of their stock, justifying it as creating stockholder value.

Big shots say 'if you can't measure it, you can't manage it'… but they can't measure their own contributions or those of the legal, accounting, and advertising groups. They are wildly against government interference or control … yet they behave so unethically that they invite more and more of it, then complain bitterly that they are handcuffed, thereby creating a never-ending and self-defeating cycle.

In government, perhaps the biggest disconnect of all was Bush I's "read my lips; no new taxes"… followed shortly by the big jump. On a smaller scale, there are the countless panderings to special-interest voters such as subsidizing sports arenas despite voters' protests … then mounting PR campaigns, complete with broad accounting numbers, to assure us that they will benefit everyone. We who can think know that they will benefit the construction unions and sports fans, most of whom will vote for the politician who robbed the tax-paying public—a group that is shrinking rapidly-- to pay special interest groups. I could write an entire book on these and similar disconnects.

And, to save what I feel is the most glaring contradiction of all for last, all BigShots, whether in government or business, are, as I've said earlier, hot for ethics…but they can't define the term and have never read a book about it. And they constantly merge and confuse ethics with law as if they are on the same level of human conduct. See APPENDIX ONE for more on this vital topic.

I've written and, if you're in business or pay any attention to the popular media, you've heard and read zillions of times that "employees are our most important assets" (if the audience is employees), and '"customers are our most important assets" (if the audience is customers). And, I'd bet the farm that those two phrases are repeated more often than any others in annual reports.

They're nice, feel-good words that have become clichés for too many BigShots and, in my mind the pinnacle of BS. However, the words are right on-- employees and customers *are* the mother lode of all other assets and are, therefore, the two most important. By far. For more on this vital topic, read *The Power of Dignity* by Pete Geissler and *Cause for Success* by Christine Arena.

The actions, which as we all know speak louder than words, are way off the words. Too often I've written those words and, a week or month later the company announces that it is downsizing or rightsizing. Both are terrible euphemisms, perfumed bull, for mass firings-- and hundreds or thousands of "valuable" employees find out that they aren't valuable at all and are discarded, many with their lives broken or grossly disrupted. The stated reasons are those awful and artful dodges for bad management: changing market conditions (isn't one function of management to anticipate and adjust to meet changing conditions?) and to increase profitability when profits are just fine. The real reasons are to cut costs and raise the value of stock options for the chosen few at the top, if only for a quarter or two.

And we hear about a company that is abandoning customers in a specific market because the return is too low and the company can invest more profitably elsewhere. I'll never forget a speech that I wrote for a CEO that he insisted, over my strenuous objections and the much weaker objections of his toady staff, he give to the thousand or so of the top execs in an industry his company had served for a century. The speech sped along these lines: We've lived off you guys for a century, you've been good to us, and

114

we've been good to you. But times have changed. (Sounds like an employee exit speech so far, eh?)

He went on: You're not paying enough for our products and services, and we demand a premium price or we won't be your supplier any longer. Why? Because we can invest in other businesses and bank a higher return.

Everybody in the room translated that threat to what it really was: extortion designed to raise the value of the CEO's and his cronies' stock options. The ploy backfired and the result wasn't pretty. The CEO raised prices across the board, customers fled to other suppliers, thousands of good and loyal employees lost their jobs, and the company went out of business…but not until the top BigShots bailed out with their golden parachutes intact.

*　　*　　*　　*　　*

If you're a CEO (an employee with special privileges that transcend ordinary company rules) who believes at some level that employees and customers are your most important assets--or if you're a lower-level employee or customer who believes that you actually are on the top of the asset hierarchy, then…

…employees can count on being meaningfully employed by a company that has a feasible plan for a viable and sustainable future, and that they are included in that plan as part of its implementation. In other words, they are not human capital, but are instead a meaningful partner. If you're a customer, you can count on your supplier for a long and continuous relationship that offers value for all parties. Too idealistic?

CHAPTER 23: BIGGER IS BETTER
Fight, Fight, for Dear Old Egomania, Part I

Bigger is Better is a close relative to Diversify or Die and Grow or Die, and all three need a bit of explaining.

Bigness, diversity, and growth aren't necessarily bull. In fact, some conditions, many beyond the control of BigShots, may demand all three. For example, unfair trade practices can give an unfair advantage to overseas firms, as they have for years to auto and steel makers, eroding core markets and forcing diversity on those firms that are the victims. To expand that thought, many analysts believe that US Steel has survived because it diversified into oil while managers streamlined steel operations at the same time, allowing it to maintain a respectable share of a flat market that was being attacked by a plethora of overseas suppliers.

Other firms have thwarted unfair trade and other practices by becoming the best in their core businesses. Whole Foods, Harley Davidson, and ALCOA—which failed in the latter part of the 1900s to broaden its aluminum core business to include "materials"—come immediately to mind. And a case can be made that IBM saved itself by expanding its mainframe computer business to PCs and, later, consulting to create a smarter world.

General Electric is perhaps the world's most diversified company, a conglomerate involved in literally hundreds of businesses. It has grown and survived in spectacular fashion, in part because of its strong leadership at the very top and the goal to be first in market share everywhere it does business.

Westinghouse, the mirror of GE in many ways, was GE's antithesis by being spectacular in its downfall. During the last half of the 1900s, it diversified into countless businesses ranging from bottled water to housing to land development to watches and commercial finance. The company claimed, proudly and loudly, that it was the world's most diversified.

Why, then, did Westinghouse dive and GE thrive? I think that a major reason was an obsession at Westinghouse to grow from good to great, to be bigger and better, to catch the GE star. This obsession led to a series of perverse decisions, perhaps the most perverse to take on highly profitable and risky second mortgages on commercial real estate.

I've seen, as you might have, the obsession with growth at any cost ruin lives and companies. In fact, I've worked with BigShots so obsessed with growth that they lost sight of reason and the longer-term consequences of their obsession. In my mind, they are idiots chasing a false god, and here's a short profile of the biggest idiot of all in my experience.

A marvelous engineer and communicator, he was promoted to VP of a global engineering/construction company. For many years, the company's revenue and profit grew methodically and responsibly, but not fast enough to satisfy ambitious new board members looking to make a killing on their stock holdings. The board also hired an outsider, the first in almost a century in business, as CEO. He was a money manipulator, not an engineer.

Rapid growth became the mantra du jour, and our VP jumped on the bandwagon with all his vigor and dedication. He negotiated contracts worth hundreds of millions at prices well below cost, hoping to make up the difference with extras--unforeseen work beyond the scope of the original contract that is usually quite profitable. Extras are a very risky way to bet on future income.

Anyway, the extras never materialized, and the company lost many millions, foundered, and finally went belly up.

Which brings me to a series of rhetorical questions.

Ask yourself: If bigger is better, why did the conglomerates of the sixties and seventies go belly up? And why isn't the Federal Government more efficient and free of graft and corruption than, say, your township? And why are the merged mega-governments of Louisville and Jacksonville struggling to create the efficiencies they promised and stay afloat? And why did Hewlett-Packard reinvent itself from a great company to a bust right after it almost doubled its size by buying Compaq over the objections of the founding families?

Then ask yourself: Is GM the leading—with its countless meanings--car manufacturer, as its ads bragged at one time, when it continuously lost market share, customer loyalty, and billions of dollars because, for many years, it produced cars with despicable reliability ratings? And why did Rick Wagoner, GM's former Chairman and CEO, reject bankruptcy in December 2005 by saying: "We don't think it's a good option." Instead, he continued, "What we need to do is get products that people are excited about and price them the right way…" Didn't he just admit that GM's products are not "leading"? And why did it take more than a century in business—and the loss of many thousands of supposedly secure jobs-- for the BigShots at GM to figure out that offering products that customers want and can afford is key to success? Isn't that business 101? And finally, why did you and I, taxpayers, bail out GM when it was on the cusp of bankruptcy?

Then ask yourself: Why is virtually ALL the growth of employment and profits attributed to small businesses, rapacious but well-managed biggies like Wal-Mart aside. And why has the number of employees in big businesses, and big unions, been declining for years, and small businesses are sprouting and thriving everywhere.

Then ask: Why do top brass at the big firms continue to spout that the company has to grow or die? Hint: Wall Street LOVES bigger and bigger numbers that they can call "growth'" so that old bugaboo, managing for stockholder value, rears its greedy head again.

The politically correct argument for Bigger is Better—the argument that the CEO puts forth in public and that I've written many times-- is that growth creates new jobs and opens up opportunities for promotion for employees that wouldn't be available otherwise. But statistics and my personal experience, and perhaps yours, prove that it's mostly bull, as you've just read.

CHAPTER 24: DIVERSIFY OR DIE
Fight, Fight, for Dear old Egomania, Part II

Q. What happened to Textron, Gulf & Western, LTV, and the other conglomerates formed during the diversification craze of the 1970s and 1980s?

A. They were killed in part by management arrogance instilled by professors at MBA programs all over the country, most of whom never met a payroll or managed a drugstore. (As is the case with Obama and many other politicians. I often wonder if that simple fact is the root cause of our endemic budget over-runs.)

Soon after World War II the Harvard Business School coined an amazingly arrogant and destructive mantra for business that went along these lines: If a manager can manage one business, he or she can manage *any or all* businesses. Other B-Schools jumped on the bandwagon, and a new generation of whiz kids was born believing that they couldn't make a bad decision if they tried, which reminds me of the play and movie, *The Producers.*

You probably remember the Whiz Kids of post World War Two – guys like Robert McNamara who actually believed that they could run any business just by playing with the accounting numbers. It worked for McNamara at Ford—some pundits credited it for saving the company from bankruptcy—but surely not at the Department of Defense, where other pundits—the same ones?-- blamed it for extending the Viet Nam war.

I felt the hubris and arrogance all the way down to my humble position as a consultant, and it always bothered me. It also was proven wrong by the failures and shrinkages of many firms.

Examples abound. Jimmy Ling springs immediately to mind, a success in the aeronautics and a bust in steel and as a conglomerator—remember LTV? Yeah, the L stands for Ling. Another is Westinghouse. It jumped on the conglomerate bandwagon and dove willy-nilly into a multitude of retail businesses and such hi-tech upstarts as hospital design in a misguided and well-intentioned effort to be more humanitarian.

One day I sat with mouth suitably agape while a young, energetic manager who came to the company with a barely used BSEE and MBA from Stanford told me that he could, using systems engineering, tell hospital administrators how their facilities could be more efficient. The company spent—I hesitate to say invested, since that would be blatant bullshit—thirty million dollars to enter a business about which it knew absolutely nothing. The company finally sunk its losses.

Westinghouse also invested more than 100 million dollars to get into the low-income, inner- city housing market, reasoning that if managers could build something as complex as a power plant they could build something so simple as a house. A few years later the business booked sales of about 180 million dollars and losses of over 200 million dollars. When I first heard those numbers I thought it was impossible for losses to exceed sales, but I was wrong. The self-proclaimed world's most diversified company was flailing and failing, and its CEO was named by a very prominent business magazine as the worst in America. One irony of that little bit of infamy is that the publisher of the magazine and the CEO were close friends. For once, the old-boy network crumbled.

I fell into the diversify trap when I bought a small stake in a restaurant. When a colleague asked why, I replied that I was not

investing in the business, I was instead investing in the manager, with whom I became friends over the several years he managed a chain restaurant near my home which I visited often.
Unfortunately, the manager knew how to run a restaurant as long as someone above him took care of the details like menu and accounting. The new restaurant went bust in fewer than two years, and I still, several years later, have not regained any confidence at all that I can judge character or expertise; I should stick to writing and teaching.

The moral is simply that there are tricks to every trade, and when managers lose sight of that they lose big bucks.

CHAPTER 25: GROW OR DIE
Fight, Fight, for Dear Old Egomania, Part III

Grow or die is a kissin' cousin to Bigger is Better and Diversify or Die, and is another scare tactic, a.k.a. the management by fear that is designed to raise the value of stock and their options held by the BigShots. The wording alone is enough to extract extra pounds of flesh and drops of blood from employees at all levels to meet unattainable, stretch goals that are painted as realistic but really aren't. The trick for the BigShots is to convince the worker bees to actually believe that the company and their jobs will die if they don't grow, i.e. increase revenues and profits.

Well, growing for the sake of growing is, far too often, the death of the business and of jobs, and I for one don't get its importance. What's the problem with being the best small company in a small market with a great and steady bottom line, loyal employees and customers, and, more importantly, staying power?

A great deal is wrong with smallness and staying power, apparently. Most companies, especially those that are publicly owned, follow a predictable pattern: They're started by an ambitious entrepreneur or entrepreneurs with a great idea—maybe you can name a company that didn't, but I can't—then grew rapidly and went public, igniting investors off on a feeding frenzy. Then growth levels out …

… but investors are still hungry and willing to flex their tyrannical power over management. So the BigShots try to bring back the good old days by diversifying away from the company's core competencies and values.

Then arrogance takes over, and the BigShots become convinced that because they became rich by managing one business they can manage any business and solve any problem with equal or greater success.

The conglomerates proved that disaster strikes at this point in the evolution. The die is cast, and the results are bankruptcies, sell-offs, and disrupted lives.

The moral: When managers become subservient to investors and their insane drive for growth, they lose their way.

Maybe Grow or Die should be Grow *and* Die.

Grow or die is akin to a personal favorite bit of bullshit: moving from good to great. Who the hell defines good? Who defines great? What are the differences between the two? The answer: profitability at any cost.

A personal story: The CEO of a big company that I consulted with often played the "good to great" tune at every opportunity, and he tried hard to convince thousands of employees that it was important to "make the transition". Although I'm sure that he held some vague idea about the meaning behind his words, he never was able to articulate it despite strong urgings from others and me to do so. In other words, there was never a measurable goal, so it was all bullshit of the foggiest kind to employees and customers. The company is no longer in business, and I'm convinced that this CEO's obsession with becoming great led to many short-term, destructive decisions.

CHAPTER 26: CREATIVITY IS REVERED
 The Blind Leading the Blind ...

Creativity is like happiness and money: more of it is good, less is bad. Trouble is, almost nobody knows what it is, which doesn't stop the BigShots from using the word at every opportunity simply because it's a good thing. So I'll help: Dr. Edward Land, of Polaroid fame, once defined creativity quite creatively as the "sudden cessation of stupidity". Dr. Margaret Mead, of sociological fame, was more expansive when she defined it as: "To the extent that a person makes, invents, or thinks something that is new to him, he is said to have performed a creative act." For Dr. Land, creativity is a happy accident; for Dr. Mead, it is a conscious act; for others it is impossible.

 Peter Georgescu, the very articulate and talented former CEO of the giant ad agency Young and Rubicam, wrote a book about the importance of creativity called *The Source of Success*. In it, he posits that creativity, a.k.a. innovation or those artful metaphors 'thinking outside the box" and "stretching the envelope", is what separates one company or person from another. In other words, creativity is the next competitive advantage for every person, company, and, yes, country, a position you'd expect from a person who has lived quite successfully by his creative wits.

Mister Georgescu goes on to say that creativity is a skill that is available to all fully engaged, normal people...it isn't reserved for the lucky few. So he agrees with Margaret Mead.

 However, he continues, "Nothing disrupts the creative process...like classic management techniques that have worked for so many centuries: bullying command-and-control, motivation through fear." Which is exactly what the larger companies continue to practice—but say they don't-- and the newer and smaller companies avoid like the bull it is.

It needn't be that way. Any firm can actually put its actions where its mouths are by fostering an environment that encourages creativity. Mister Georgescu describes such an environment very nicely: clear and measurable goals and aspirations; a supportive culture that provides the needed information to creative persons and teams and allows for risk-taking and its inevitable failures and rejections; and financial and psychic rewards for measurable results.

He should know. Ad agencies are arguably the most successful of all organizations in fostering creativity, simply because they must. Any agency's survival depends on a continuous flow of new ideas that broadcast clients' messages most compellingly, the form of bull that we have become accustomed to and hardened against, and that I addressed earlier.

The Creative Department is perhaps unique to ad agencies, as is "creative" in the titles of certain revered employees. The Creative Director is esteemed for his or her abilities to come up with the grand ideas that clients approve and pay for, and that actually sell products. Everyone benefits.

I asked a BigShot or two why, if creativity is so revered, their firms don't have a creative department, a manager of creativity. I was told that every department is creative in its own way. OK, but why not bring the word out of the closet?

A friend mused the other day: What would happen if all employees of a firm were told that their jobs and salary were guaranteed for a year, and that all would share equally in the growth in profits at the end of the year, forming a mini-socialist society with maxi-capitalist rewards. Would it unleash creativity? Would it discourage creativity of the few who are most creative? If so, would the less—or more-- creative become resentful? Would it mimic 1984, the book, and stymie creativity almost entirely? Would it unleash creativity in a small firm but not in a larger? The questions went on, ad infinitum, ad nauseum. You decide if you'd like to try it; if you do, I'd like to help you.

CHAPTER 27: DOWNSIZING IS OUR SALVATION
  It's Rarely Worked, so Let's ...

Downsizing is, as everyone knows by now, perfumed language for firing all sorts of employees--but never the top guys and their cronies-- in order to cut costs and inflate the value of stock and stock options held by the same top brass.

As is the case with Bigger is Better, the BS lies in the rationale: Downsizing is needed to save the company, which is almost always blatant BS for two reasons. First, most of the time the company is just going through a rough patch and profits are down a bit for the short term. The company isn't even close to being on the cusp of going under, but the stock price will wallow at lower levels for a while and that's bad for the BigShots' portfolios and egos, especially for those about to retire.

Second, stats show conclusively that companies, after an initial drop in costs and rise in profits, actually perform *worse after downsizing* than they did before.

 Hmmm...maybe employees really *are* valuable assets!

The entire idea and process of downsizing reminds me of a marketing manager I know well who, perplexed, came to me--a writer with a flair for sales, marketing, and cutting through the fog of bull-- to analyze why sales were dropping when the market was expanding and his products were competitive. I reminded him that his boss, only a few months before, decreed a ten percent "head-count reduction" (another abominable cover-up for human carnage and a huge error in planning for the future), and a comparable cut in the advertising budget—regardless of their contributions to sales and profits. He didn't see the direct correlation, or, more accurately, he didn't *want* to see it.

Is that mindless denial, or what?

"Downsize" has been replaced by "rightsize"; it's more politically correct—it sounds better, but isn't, so it's classic bull. Both terms are cover-ups for management's failure to prepare for the future, its primary task.

CHAPTER 28: STRATEGIC PLANNING AND SPIN
Another Advertisement for ...

Strategic planning is, supposedly, a blueprint for the long-term future of the total business, including its employees and customers. As such, it is totally at odds with managing for stockholder value, which literally demands short-term decisions that benefit the biggest of the BigShots and destroy the troops.

"Spin" is what we writers call "surgical writing", i.e. we select what we want to say (benefits the sender of the message, the client) and reject what we don't want to say (harms the sender). So the receiver of the message gets a biased, one-sided picture, which is true of messages in newspapers and magazines as well as brochures, ads, and speeches by Big Shots in all walks of life. Spin is everywhere, and of course it spits in the eye of ethics/honesty/integrity/ truth, but...

...how is it related to strategic planning? Well, strategic plans—a term that is either a redundancy or an oxymoron depending on your point of view—are the ultimate spins (and you thought ads and brochures are!). The reasons: their real purposes are to paint the business in the best possible light, requiring that bad news be sliced away in order to attract the funds needed to grow or die, diversify or die, or play bigger is better. Unfortunately, this bias results far too often in bad or marginal investments and, instead of grow, the result is die, usually slowly and painfully. Ugh.

Also, I've written dozens of strategic plans and they *all* are financial projections; they are so internally focused—read self-centered or egocentric or, at best, sociocentric—that they *never* mention employees, customers, suppliers, or communities. So much, again, for our "most important assets".

A personal experience: I was lunching with a VP Marketing after a quick golf game at my club, the dues for which were hidden in my fees, so his company paid them but didn't want to know it. The game and lunch combined into a gift of more than three hundred dollars, which of course violated his company's Code of Ethics. He should have been fired for accepting it; I can tell you neither he nor I gave it a thought.

Our conversation moved somehow to long-range or strategic planning. He laughed: "Long-range planning is deciding where to go to lunch. We spend millions of dollars each year on planning and then, after the top brass approve the documents, they're put on the shelf to collect dust and we go about our business as usual—hitting our financial goals for the month."

Two anecdotes demonstrate the point further. I helped the president of a hi-tech company to put together a plan and then a speech to explain it to employees. When I pointed out that the plan was nothing more than financial projections and never mentioned the employees and customers needed to pull it off, I was fired for my insolence.

I also helped the general manager of a large division to justify spending millions to move the business from a cold to warm climate—I warned you up-front that I was an enabler of bullshit. The rationale for the move was so thin that I can't believe that the board accepted it, but I was underestimating the unstoppable power of cronyism. The real reason for the move was simply that this GM was a dedicated sailor and was three years away from retirement. The lure of a free move, both for him and his yacht, was irresistible.

The President of a small engineering/consulting firm learned in MBA school that he needed a strategic plan if he were to succeed. He didn't learn how to write one, so, after struggling with it for a year, hired me to "pull it all together." I did, and recommended that he share it will all employees to help assure that they were working toward common goals. A year or so later, the Manager of Engineering, concerned about his future and management succession, asked me if the plan had been written, and was astounded when I told him that it had been. Seems that the plan was put on the shelf … another example of a BigShot who can't walk the talk.

CHAPTER 29: FADS/ MANTRAS
The Bandwagon Plays On, and On, and On ...

I love to see my clients latch on to the latest fad; I make a lot of money helping them to communicate and justify it to the masses of employees and to stock analysts as "good for the company and its owners, our stockholders."

I've lived through Productivity, the mantra of the 1970s that became perfumed language for downsizing or rightsizing millions of dedicated employees to cut costs and to squeeze more work from those who are already overworked.

It was followed quickly by Quality, when managers realized that the Japanese and other overseas manufacturers had replaced the vile and self-serving, self-defeating "planned obsolescence" with products that performed reliably for many years. Productivity and Quality were rolled into one mantra called Total Quality Management, which was refined into Six Sigma, which was embraced by Neutron Jack Welch and GE and so became the Apex of Aphorisms for all the sheep to follow.

Then along came Supply Chain Management, Speed, and Information as competitive advantages, and a bunch of subdivisions: Re-engineering, Paradigm Shift, Restructuring, Continuous Learning, ad infinitum and ad nauseum.

All of the mantras de jour spawned armies of consultants de jour, which in turn spawned huge mounds of bullshit guaranteed to save or give wondrous advantages to any manager willing to listen and adopt and adapt. Just one example: A consultant wrote a small book about the need to recognize Paradigm Shifts in order to plan ahead. He never told the poor reader what such a shift is or what it might look or feel like, or why anyone should give a shit. In fact, the entire book was one thought written as a multitude of varied sentences: Recognize and plan for paradigm shifts or die.

What will be the Next Big Mantra? I don't know, but I suspect that it will be sustainability, a remarkably malleable buzzword that I try to explain in APPENDIX C. The word began in the environmental movement and t is now freighted with too many meanings to count, so it's the perfect vehicle for obfuscation by those who are best at it, the advertising and PR agencies, like me, and in-house departments. I do know that I'll make big bucks explaining it to "change the culture" of my clients' organizations, and that my explanations will sustain (sic) the same old bullshit.

All of this jumping on the latest fad is a fallacy of thinking called *bandwagoning*. The fallacy argues that a position is valid or correct because a number of people share the same belief. Yet, conformity to a belief is often destructive because what others think can be right or wrong, strong or weak, real or fantasy. Think about that when our governments at all levels act on the basis of polls rather than independent and clear thinking, and is justified with such pomposity as reacting to the wishes and needs of constituents, which of course is another plea to be reelected.

History is replete with examples. Perhaps the most glaring in history and politics is the German public jumping on the Hitler bandwagon; in business it might be planned obsolescence or, more recently, stockholder value which morphed into stakeholder value. Others include jumping on the dot com boom of the 1990s and the irrational exuberance it spawned in the financial markets, and alternative fuels such as ethanol or hydrogen as steps toward that impossible dream called energy independence. In the fuzzy realms of politics and science, the bandwagoning continues by being absolutely certain that carbon is the cause of global warming when so many other factors are involved, and in the insane idea that our society is sustainable when nobody can define the term.

All this does not mean that managers should not look for and adopt new management concepts and techniques; they should, and they are swamped by too many from which to pick and choose. The world changes, it seems, at an increasingly fast and bewildering pace, and that fact alone requires Agile Adaptation (is that another fad that screams for a complete book by itself?). However, Agile Adaptation does not mean that managers should abandon fundamental concepts that have proven to be effective over time. In fact, those concepts are needed more than ever in a changing world; they create the stability and staying power that are so badly needed in our Age of Anxiety.

If you want to read more about this awful fallacy, pick up a copy of *Extraordinary Popular Delusions and the Madness of Crowds,* by Charles Mackay, and *Tulipomania, The Story of the World's Most Coveted Flower,* by Mike Dash.

"There's always an easy solution to every problem—neat, plausible and wrong."
  H. L. Mencken

CHAPTER 30: MY EMPLOYEES MUST WRITE BETTER
I Don't Know Why, but ...

I admit up front that I am biased big-time against this particular bit of bull; I garner significant fees for teaching employees to write, so readers may construe this entire chapter as a self-serving gripe. Nevertheless, the bullshit is rampant and true, as the following anecdotes demonstrate.

A partner of a huge consulting firm called, told me how concerned he was with the quality of his firm's proposals and reports, asked what I could do to improve them. I explained my seminars and their costs. He thanked me, and then purchased hundreds of new computers, one for each employee who writes. He spent far more than he would have for my seminars, and absolutely guaranteed that the bad writing that he was so concerned about would remain bad—computers do not improve the quality of writing; only the human brain can do that. But computers guarantee that bad writing, and its many profit-busting effects, will be transmitted more rapidly.

A CEO of a large construction firm announced in his State-of-the-Company speech that he gives every January that his #1 initiative for the year was to improve every employee's writing, which he described, quite correctly, as "abominable and disgraceful". One of his top execs immediately contacted me, asked me to send the CEO information on my seminars. I did, and followed up with additional information several times over the ensuing six months. The CEO didn't respond, and has done absolutely nothing for the past 18 months to advance his #1 initiative. Walk the talk? Don't be silly. An aside that I find astonishing: not one employee has challenged the CEO to follow through. Do you think that this firm is managed by fear? Do you think the employees care about improving their writing?

The President of a mid-size engineering company called to ask about my seminars and soon after actually retained me for one series. He was pleased with the results, and, about a year later, asked me to propose more classes. I did, and he did nothing: "We're doing OK but could do better", he explained, "and, besides, I'll retire in a few months." I call that the "even keel conundrum" which, translated, means that when business is good we can't be bothered with anything as strategic as better writing, and when business is bad, we can't take time away from sales efforts.

In fairness, I have clients who walk the talk. I've completed at least six series of seminars –at least 120 two-hour classes--for a firm of only 35 people; the President has noted that everyone has benefitted, and business is thriving. The execs at a larger firm have retained me to teach more than 150 of their 500 employees, some in distant offices. They see and are pleased with the results.

On a broader scale, I have written a dozen or so articles and two books that address the benefits of good writing. Many execs agree that my points are valid, muse that they need to act on them, and then move on to the next emergency. I think that they are looking for the quick fix to a problem that they don't or won't understand. I see similarities with strategic planning.

For more, read The Power of Writing Well, by Pete Geissler, and ponder these words:

"Words are, of course, the most powerful drugs used by mankind."
Rudyard Kipling.

APPENDIX A: MORE ON LAW AND ETHICS FROM AN ETHICIST

Rushworth M. Kidder is founder and president of the Institute of Global Ethics, and a fascinating and engaging writer. In his book, *How Good People Make Tough Choices,* he discusses law and ethics in this way:

Law and ethics are not the same. Yet it should go without saying that obedience to law, while it is usually a necessary condition for ethical action, is not sufficient to guarantee it. Individuals who merely obey the letter of the law may or may not be ethical. That point is nicely made whenever the Ethics Committee of the United States Senate determines that because one of its members has broken no regulation, he or she is considered ethical. The widespread cynicism over some of the committee's determinations suggests that public faith in that misnamed body, which appears to have no interest in "ethics"... but only in laws or regulations that may have been violated.

Obeying the law, then, is not enough to earn the "ethical" label.

Mr. Kidder continues on this theme in another part of his book:

...the old adage, if it ain't illegal, it must be ethical, is so deeply flawed. Ethics and law ... are as different as the unenforceable from the enforceable. To be sure, law is a kind of condensation of ethics into codification: it reflects areas of moral agreement so broad that the society comes together and says, "This ethical behavior shall be mandated."...When ethics collapses, the law rushes in to fill the void. Why? Because regulation is essential to sustain any kind of human experience involving two or more people. The choice is not, "Will society be regulated?" The choice

138

*is only between unenforceable self-regulation and enforceable
regulation...Surely a powerful indicator of ethical decay is the glut
of new laws—and new lawyers—spilling into the market each year.
If ... our ethical decay is severe, the age of hyper-regulation
cannot be far behind.*

Hyper regulation scares every business BigShot because their
power, and their incomes, would decrease. On the other hand, it
energizes most, maybe every, government BigShot because their
power and incomes would increase. In short, the balance of power
would shift to government, which is initially called socialism, and
eventually communism. Business BigShots deplore the very idea,
yet they behave as if they love it.

 I'm reminded here of Norman Cousins' words: "Government in
the U.S. today is a senior partner in every business in the country."
And I'm reminded of Winston Churchill's words: "The inherent
vice of capitalism is the unequal sharing of blessings; the inherent
virtue of socialism is the equal sharing of miseries."

*APPENDIX B: DECEITFUL FIGURES OF SPEECH THAT
BULLSHITTERS ADORE*

We all revert to various figures of speech to add color or interest to
our words, and that's legitimate. We also use them to create
bullshit, and that is illegitimate. For example, Big Shots likely
became BigShots at least in part because they communicate well
(have a way with words), and stay BigShots for the same reason.

BigShots are addicted to:

Euphemism is the art of replacing an offensive word or phrase
with one that is more socially acceptable, avoiding a harsh or
unpleasant reality. Euphemism is fine when used to be more polite
or tactful or diplomatic to spare the sensibilities of others. For
example, we use "passed away" instead of "died"; "slept with" or
"had a relationship with' instead of "had sex with" (or countless
other more vulgar terms which we reserve for more vulgar
settings); "got sick" instead of "threw up"; and so on with such
phrases as "powder my nose" and "go to the rest room" for the
normal bodily functions that we can't mention in polite company.

Euphemism becomes bull shit when it is used to deceive.
Examples abound in this book: the endemic downsizing or
rightsizing instead of firing for all the wrong reasons; "I could
have been more forthright" for "I lied to you earlier" or "I
misspoke" for "I lied", and "our earnings declined for conditions
beyond our control" for "I failed to see the changes coming, which
of course is a failure of my management duties".

Jargon is so pervasive that it deserves a chapter of its own. See
CHAPTER TWELVE.

Bureaucratese is the piling on of words upon words, the more words with the more syllables and the longer the sentences the better, because the purpose of bureaucratese is to overwhelm the audience with volume and pomposity. Examples include economists calling a recession "a period of negative economic growth", and this from a research report" Opportunity Review: Method for Nox Adsorber Desulfation in a Multi-path Exhaust System",, which could have been: "Opportunity Review: A new way to remove nitrogen from auto exhausts." And this from a BigShot: "Our approach of continuous improvement drives us forward from this point and we are sure you agree that expenditure forecasting and budget management are key elements in managing the profitability of any business, no matter what the size of the organization." Readers could have understood what this pompous windbag meant if he had written: "We will continue to improve our profitability with more accurate budgeting and control over expenditures."

Rhetoric is simply artificial and artful language designed to impress or persuade, too often with tinges of exaggeration or insincerity. Rhetoric often takes the form of a question that assumes the answer preferred by the questioner in order to lead the listener or reader to the proper conclusion. In other words, rhetoric is designed to create agreement with the speaker/writer, and is used indiscriminately by politicians and businesspeople of all stripes. A good example in business is the BigShot who justifies his or her exorbitant compensation with this query: "You want the best talent available to run your company, don't you?" The answer must be "yes"—nobody but an idiot would want bad talent at the top—but neither the question nor the answer is related to the issue, which is "Is the BigShot the best talent available, and is he/she being compensated fairly?" By the way, a rhetorical question is not the same as a trick question, which is best exemplified by that old legal twist: "When did you stop beating your wife?" Or in the same vein, "When did you stop robbing banks?" (Or shareholders.)

Oxymoron is the juxtaposition of terms that may seem true or plausible but could just as easily be contradictory or implausible. When used by bull shitters, oxymorons are designed to confuse and obfuscate reality. The classic examples include military intelligence and Minister of Information, the title Hitler, perhaps history's most adept user of bullshit, bestowed on Josef Goebbels, whose duties were to dispense misinformation, a.k.a. propaganda. Then there's "fiscal responsibility" to hide budgets that are out of control and all sorts of other financial manipulations, and this from an engineering report: "The positive side of negative pressure." Perhaps the most damaging is this from Wall Street: *Long Term Capital Management*, the name of the huge hedge fund that went bust back in 1996. It has nothing to do with long term or management, but a lot about capital for its principles.

APPENDIX C: WORDS THAT SIGNAL THAT BULL IS ON ITS WAY

1. *Sustainable,* adjective, and its derivative, sustainability, noun and adverb, all of which have been used in so many ways beyond the simple "continuing" that they have lost all meaning.
2. *Progressive* sounds like a good thing no matter how it's used, but, in my experience, is always a modern euphemism for socialism, communism, and fascism: bigger, more controlling government.
3. *Statistically proven* or demonstrated; anyone can prove whatever he or she wants by merely tweaking assumptions and the reader/listener will never know.
4. *Bolder, brighter, faster, better* and the like without substantial support as to why and how.
5. *I misspoke, I wasn't forthcoming, I misled* and other more polite, politically correct euphemisms for outright lying.
6. *Crisis,* which has been so over-worked that its meaning- a severe situation—has been diluted. Nevertheless, Big Shots continue to use it to attract attention of a complacent audience, often to extract funds for a per project.

APPENDIX D: REALITY REPRISED

Most employees who have moved up in an organization above the very lowest levels know the difference between being convinced and bullshitted in some part of their psyches. To explain, they are either consciously aware of the difference and are visibly pissed off--a small percentage, I fear-- or they feel vaguely uncomfortable and angry with the message or its delivery--a much larger percentage, but certainly not the remainder. The rest, probably 55 to 60 percent of us, don't give a shit—which is about the same percentage of our population that doesn't vote but feels compelled to bitch about the results anyway, a contradiction of major proportions. (Are *concerned voter* and *concerned stockowner* oxymorons?)

So, dear and intelligent reader, what does all this mean to you? Just this: reality is the antidote to bullshit, and reality is good business. Which raises the question: How do you create reality?

Well, in its abstract, reality is created in two ways: We report events as they actually are and disclose important truths (we're accurate); and we report what we know about the subject (we're as complete and balanced as we need to be to state the actual situation).

These principles—accuracy, completeness, and balance—can be demonstrated by a true story of two parts, the first called What took place; the second What could have taken place in the same situation.

First, here's what took place, and I am not joking. A major corporation was obviously going bust or close to it, and employees, suppliers, customers, and the top guys in city government were

144

nervous about their sources of income. The bad news was everywhere in the media, obvious to anybody who could read or listen, but the last shoe hadn't dropped and most folks hoped for a miracle that would pull the fat from the fire. Their hope wasn't totally unfounded: the company had survived a number of similarly serious crises—wouldn't that raise bright red flags about the competency of management?—during its century-long history, the most recent only about 30 years earlier and fresh in the memories of many.

On top of the dismal finances was equally dismal morale, which led to very dismal drops in productivity, which, in an inevitable chain, caused the even more dismal finances. Losses of billions piled up on losses of more billions, and employees spent more time tuning up their resumes than tuning up their job performances.

So the Prez called in his VP of communications and they mapped out a campaign to visit the company's 50 or so locations for all-employee meetings, a huge productivity dropper and expense. Then they put together a pretty slick, a.k.a. expensive, dog and pony show with all sorts of graphs and charts (smoke and mirrors) to prove that, yes, the company is down a bit, but fret not, the trouble was fixable by the wonderful management team that was in place at headquarters…

…if only everyone sacrificed by, for example, cutting travel and entertainment expenses to only those which were "essential". Which always puzzled me: aren't all expenses essential to meet some purpose, and, if they're not, why were they incurred and why did management approve them?

Well, the reaction of employees was exactly what you'd expect:

Disgust and disdain from those who knew the realities. I heard countless comments along the lines of "they ask us to cut expenses and they show up here with an entourage and a show that costs more than I make in a year, all to throw bullshit at what we know to be a serious problem."

The Prez and his VP underestimated the intelligence of their audience.

Here's what could—should? -- have taken place, in these steps:

1. The Prez sits down with his top financial officer and outlines the real situation in a few simple sentences, then…
2. He meets with his four executive VPs to discuss the best strategies to create long-term solvency and employment, *i.e. the continuity of the firm*, not short-term profitability, and the five of them outline their decisions in a few sentences. Examples:

    -I will cut the compensation of all top managers by ten percent and terminate my morale-busting relationship with your VP communications.

    -John X will personally manage AAA division, the biggest loser in his portfolio, and return it to profitability in six months without cutting employment. His actions will…

    -And so on, with specific responsibilities and schedules clearly spelled out.
3. Points one and two are sent via email to all employees, even the janitors, and all board members, stockholders, and business editors. The emails ask for reactions and suggestions.
4. Progress reports in a similar format are emailed to the same persons every two weeks, and substantive replies, far more than 'thanks for your suggestions', are emailed to all persons who submit reactions and suggestions.

I ask you: If that had taken place, wouldn't management have created a sense of shared purpose--to save the firm and everyone's job? Wouldn't all employees have been more willing to sacrifice a bit? Wouldn't the firm have had a better chance of surviving?

It didn't; it drowned in its own bullshit that was fueled by arrogance and greed.

The slow and painful death of Westinghouse was undeniable proof that more empires die from internal corruption and short-sightedness—I almost wrote 'stupidity' here, but didn't because the BigShots all have high IQs and low savvy—than from external forces.

Westinghouse died for many reasons that can be generalized as misdirected, misguided management—basically an insane drive for ever-increasing quarterly profits, which led to all sorts of operating and accounting manipulations. One example of many: plant managers would ship incomplete or improperly tested equipment in order to book the sales and profits now, knowing full well that the costs to complete the order and fix the defects could very well wipe out the profit at a later date.

The result of this and other feel-good machinations was losses in the billions, which eventually sunk the company, unnecessarily. Yes, the BigShots could have saved the company if their egos hadn't gotten in the way. A larger competitor offered to buy the risky loans at a discount, halting the bloodletting with one substantial, but not fatal, write-off. The big shots refused; their arrogance wouldn't let the biggest quarterly loss, and the biggest loss of stock price, in the history of the firm take place on their watch, and they wanted to protect their options—self-interest that turned out to be self-destruction.

Bullshit clashes with reality on many levels in every organization. A marketing manager I know well was negotiating a multi-million-dollar deal with a big company in Spain, and apparently coming in second. Then the marketing manager with the leading bidder made a huge mistake: he sent a letter to the chief purchasing agent detailing the many faults of my friend's offer, and the purchasing agent asked my friend to respond. Was it ethical to pass along a letter to a competitor when the letter might have been considered confidential? Shouldn't the purchaser have determined for himself the truth or bull supporting each point? Wasn't the purchaser pitting one bias against another?

Regardless of your answers to those queries, my friend, sensing an opening, responded in writing, point by point, explaining in great and supportable detail the fallacies behind each. Several points, in fact, were about a third bidder's offer, and others indicated total unawareness of the technology involved and its evolution over the years. You could say that the letter was bull shit based on ignorance.

The result was that reality triumphed and my friend got the order.

My former stockbroker is another example of refreshing reality. He at one time would recommend investments that were touted by his firm's analysts. When I pointed out to him that many of the recommendations turned out to be under performers, he, to my surprise, agreed. Then he explained further: Analysts too often recommend investments that the firm has in inventory and must be sold regardless of merit or value, or that pay bigger commissions to the brokers and managers up the line. It all boiled down to money, not clients' welfare. Then he said something that I never expected: He suggested that I find a good money manager who was unaffiliated with a brokerage, enabling him or her to operate more objectively.

I did, my broker became my former broker and one of my best friends, and I rest more easily as my portfolio grows nicely.

FURTHER READING

On Corporate BullShit:

The Dictionary of Corporate Bullshit, by Lois Beckwith

The Business of Bullshit, by Graham Edmonds

Dictionary of Bullshit, by Nick Webb

Why Businesspeople Sound Like Idiots, by Brian Fugere, Chelsea Hardaway, and Jon Warshawsky

Your Call is Important to Us, by Laura Penny

Double Speak, by William Lutz

On the Fallacies of Predictions:

State of Fear, by Michael Crichton

Unstoppable Global Warming: Every 1500 Years, by Dr. Fred Singer

Shattered Consensus, by Dr. Patrick Michaels

Useless Arithmetic: Why Environmental Scientists Can't Predict the Future, by Orrin H.   Pilkey and Linda Pilkey-Jarvis

Gusher of Lies: The Dangerous Delusion of Energy Independence, by Robert Bryce

On Ethics:

How Good People Make Tough Choices, by Rushmore Kidder

Moral Courage, by Rushmore Kidder

The Power of Dignity, by Pete Geissler

On the Lack of Ethics:

Corporate Abuse, by Lesley Wright and Marti Smye

On Thinking and Problem-Solving:

The Rational Manager: A Systematic Approach to Problem-Solving and Decision-Making, by Charles H. Kepner and Benjamin B. Tregoe

The Lessons of History, by Will and Ariel Durant

The Power of Being Articulate, by Pete Geissler

Genius, by Harold Bloom

Thinker Toys, by Michael Michalko

On Managing for Core Values:

The Bible

Cause for Success: 10 Companies that Put Profits Second and Came in First, by Christine Arena

Built to Last: Successful Habits of Visionary Companies, by James C. Collins and Jerry Porres

The Fifth Discipline, by Peter Senge

Peak, by Chip Conley